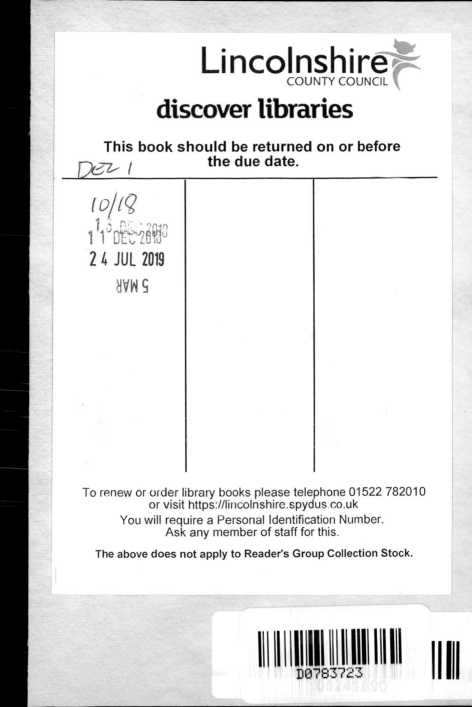

Lincolnshire
COUNTY COUNCIL

discover libraries

This book should be returned on or before the due date.

DEC 1

10/18

13 DEC 2010

1 1 DEC 2010

2 4 JUL 2019

5 MAR

THE CURIOUS

BARTENDER'S

GUIDE

TO

GIN

THE CURIOUS

BARTENDER'S
GUIDE
TO
GIN

TRISTAN STEPHENSON

RYLAND PETERS & SMALL
LONDON • NEW YORK

Designers Geoff Borin and Emily Breen
Editors Nathan Joyce and Gillian Haslam
Production Manager Gordana Simakovic
Picture Manager Christina Borsi
Art Director Leslie Harrington
Editorial Director Julia Charles
Publisher Cindy Richards

Prop Stylist Sarianne Plaisant
Indexer Hilary Bird

Originally published as *The Curious Bartender's Gin Palace* in 2016,
this abridged and retitled edition first published in 2018 by
Ryland Peters & Small
20–21 Jockey's Fields
London WC1R 4BW
and
341 E 116th St
New York NY 10029

www.rylandpeters.com

10 9 8 7 6 5 4 3 2 1

Text © Tristan Stephenson 2016, 2018

Design and commissioned photography by Addie Chinn © Ryland
Peters & Small 2016, 2018 (see page 192 for full picture credits)

ISBN: 978-1-78879-039-0

A CIP record for this book is available from the British Library.
US Library of Congress CIP data has been applied for.

Printed in China

CONTENTS

INTRODUCTION

Even before I was old enough to drink gin, I was thinking about it. My earliest memory of gin is my mother drinking a gin and tonic when I was nine, and, as it looked like a glass of lemonade, I thought it only right that I should be allowed one too. Even today I am known to react badly when refused a gin and tonic so my parents pacified me with a glass of tonic water. From the first sip I fell in love with its tongue-curling bitterness and that night I sneaked down to the kitchen and greedily swigged straight from a bottle. It would be a few more years before I could mix it with gin of course, but there was never any question that this heavenly mix of the sweet, bitter, boozy and botanical would become a big feature in my adult life.

Of course I never would have guessed that it would become this much of a feature. The most significant step was becoming a bartender, but when I got better at that I found myself delivering seminars on gin and judging gin competitions. Later, I appeared in advertising for a major gin brand, and opened two London cocktail bars – both heavily inspired by gin. After that I co-founded a (small) gin brand, and now I've written a gin book, having visited over 60 gin distilleries and sampled nearly 500 expressions. You could say I'm 'ginfatuated'.

And for good reason, too. In gin we have a spirit that is so specific in its flavouring, so chilling in its reputation, yet so far-reaching in its contribution to cocktails and mixed drinks.

From its origins as a medieval medicinal curative to becoming one of the world's first recreational spirits, gin, and its Dutch precursor, genever, soon became the go-to tipple for the British masses in the early 18th century. To say that party got out of hand would be playing it down somewhat. Juniper-scented gut-rot flowed through the streets of London, leading the poor and vulnerable into harm's

way. But out of the ashes, something unexpected happened, and in the space of 100 years, gin journeyed from the backstreet bar rooms of London's inner-city slums to the cocktail lists of the most exclusive hotels in the world. Indeed, gin was the cocktail spirit, engulfing whiskey and brandy in a cloud of juniper-scented smoke by the beginning of the 20th century. Hundreds of dry gin cocktails were masterminded between 1900–1930. Not least of all, the Martini.

There is something about a Martini,
A tingle remarkably pleasant;
A yellow, a mellow Martini;
I wish I had one at present.
There is something about a Martini,
Ere the dining and dancing begin,
And to tell you the truth,
It is not the vermouth
I think that perhaps it's the gin.

A Drink With Something In It by Ogden Nash

Who could have guessed that in the 50 years that followed, gin's fortunes would change once again, fading away in to mediocrity becoming neither celebrated nor feared, but just unremarkable. The 1980s saw some of gin's most woeful times, where the cocktails of the golden era had been forgotten only to be replaced by vodka and a new era of cocktail culture where the concealment of a spirit's character through liberal use of sugar and fruit was the primary goal. Only gin's loyalest disciples kept the gin dream alive. Refusing to part company with their gin and tonics, keeping the fire burning and the ice stirring from bar room to home liquor cabinet.

Gin, as it stands today, occupies a curious position within the hearts and minds of drinkers. On the one hand there is 'mother's ruin', the degenerative scourge of 18th-century English men and women, which has resonated through the centuries. On the other hand, though, gin has become a highly prized pinup of the craft revolution. Eschewing gin today is like sticking a finger up to local, artisan, independent businesses.

But the range of styles has also helped to a garner new admirers too. Assume the barstool position in any bar with a decent gin range and it won't be long until you hear that familiar sentence, 'I didn't used to like gin, but I like this one', signifying a new breed of gin drinker whose preconceptions have been squashed like a wedge of fresh lime. Pronounced flavour, credible provenance, botanical terroir and innovative packaging are just some of considerations that drive modern gin drinkers to buy one brand over another. This isn't just a renaissance of gin that we are experiencing right now – it's gin's golden time. Gin has never been this good and it might never be this good again, so enjoy it while you can, and be sure to enjoy this book with your gin drink of choice firmly in your hand.

THE HISTORY OF GIN

ALCHEMY, MAGIC AND THE ORIGINS OF DISTILLATION

Some scholars believe that it was the Chinese who first unearthed the secrets of distillation and that their findings were shared with Persian, Babylonian, Arabian and Egyptian merchants through centuries of trade along the old silk routes that penetrated into the Middle East. These 3,200-km (2,000-mile) trails became well established in the 2nd century BC, and were used to trade gold, jade, silk and spices. However, it was as a hub of cultural networking that the silk route really came in to its own. It was, in effect, the information superhighway of its time.

Whether the Chinese got the know-how from the Indo-Iranian people, or the other way around, the mystic of ardent waters and

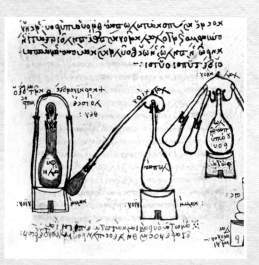

LEFT The first alembic stills designed by Zosimos of Panoplis use the same basic design as those made today.

botanical vapours was seething up in to the classical civilizations, where the preeminent physicians, alchemists and botanists took great interest in it.

The Greek philosopher Aristotle was certainly aware of distillation in one shape or another. One section of his *Meteorologica* (circa 340 BC) concerns experiments that he undertook to distil liquids, discovering that 'wine and all fluids that evaporate and condense in to a liquid state become water.'

In 28 BC a practising magi known as Anaxilaus of Thessaly was expelled from Rome for performing his magical arts, which included setting fire to what appeared to be water. The secrets of the trick were later translated in to Greek and published in around 200 AD by Hippolytus, presbyter of Rome – it turned out he used distilled wine. Around the same time Pliny the Elder experimented with hanging fleeces above cauldrons of bubbling resin, and using the expansive surface area of the wool to catch the vapour and condense it in to turpentine. Could Pliny have experimented with juniper distillates? Perhaps. But if he did, he didn't tell us.

The world's first self-proclaimed alchemist, Zosimos, an Gnostic mystic from Egypt, was also thought to be somewhat of a wizard with alcohol. He provided one of the first definitions of alchemy as the study of 'the composition of waters, movement, growth, embodying and disembodying, drawing the spirits from bodies and bonding the spirits within bodies.' It was Zosimos' belief that distillation in some way liberates the essence of a body or object that has lead to our definition of alcoholic beverages as 'spirits' today.

Up and until at least 900 AD these studies in spirit and alcohol were confined to the Middle East. Europe was still wallowing in a kind of post-Roman Empire hangover that had been dragging on for the better part of half a millennium. And while the Europeans passed the time burning witches and sharpening steel, Islam erected the Great Mosques of Damascus and Samarra, and bred scholars and scientists. Under the ruling of the caliphate Muslim borders expanded, and so too did schools of mathematics, alchemy and medicine. During that time Abu Musa Jabir ibn Hayyan (who, in time, became known simply as Geber) emerged, in what stands as modern day Iraq, as the undisputed father of distillation. It was the research and observations of Geber that established the fundamental understanding of distillation throughout Islamic culture.

With knowledge came power, and the Moors (a Muslim group from north Africa) persistently and systematically seized big chunks of southern Europe from the 8–9th centuries: Spain, Portugal, parts of southern France and Malta all fell to a force that was superior in every way.

In the 11th century the Europeans began to claw their way back however. Ranks were formed, the Catholic church rallied, and very slowly the 'Reconquista' groaned into action. But this was a lengthy process, leaving some cities, like Toledo in Spain, under Muslim occupation for over 300 years. Once the Europeans moved in and noticed the rather impressive libraries, and the surprisingly well-educated people that inhabited the lands they had seized, the thirst for education and enlightenment became the new focus.

Universities of learning were established and one of them, Schola Medica Salernitana, in Salerno, Italy, would play an important role in the development of distillation. At that time the Principality of Salerno covered almost the entire western coast of southern Italy. Salerno had unprecedented access to Arabic materials thanks to regular interaction with the Byzantines (who liked nothing better than warring with the Arabs and Ottomans), but more importantly the Moors, who occupied Sicily from 902 AD through to the end of the 11th century, and regular skirmishes on to the Italian mainland would have taken them right up to the doorstep of Schola Medica Salernitana.

ABOVE For the curious
12th-century physician, there
was no better place to hone
your craft than Salerno's
medical school.

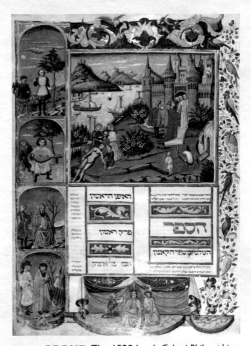

ABOVE The 1529 book *Geberi Philosophi ac
Alchimistae Maximi, de Alchimia Libri Tres* features
the works of pioneering alchemist Geber.

One of the school's primary functions was translation work from
Arabic or Greek into Latin. Arabic or Hebrew would be translated
into Castilian by Muslim and Jewish scholars, and from Castilian
into Latin by Castilian scholars. Knowledge blossomed. The
scholars of antiquity who presided over this – Johannes Platearius,
Bartholomew and Michael Salernus – outputted reams of material
during the school's golden era, and within the dense volumes
of their work we find the first inquisitions into distillation by
Europeans. One recipe book of herbal treatments, which was
originally compiled by Platearius at some point in the 12th century,
even includes a recipe for a tonic distilled from wine mixed with
squashed juniper berries.

THE HISTORY OF
MEDICINAL JUNIPER

Juniper has consistently been one of the most widely used trees in the whole of human history. It was essential to the survival of some primitive cultures who used the wood as a material to construct shelter, or shaped it into utensils, weapons and furniture, or who simply burned it to provide heat and light. Societies have fed themselves with juniper (some Native American tribes were known to consume juniper berries in something resembling a fried juniper burger – I wouldn't advise trying it) and even the Bible makes reference to juniper as food, in Job (30:4) the King describes the desperation of his impoverished subjects as they 'cut up juniper roots for meat'. It lends itself better to being sustenance for livestock, and juniper is widely grown for decoration and landscaping purposes, and is a firm favourite of the bonsai tree-growing community.

THE WONDER-DRUG OF THE UNDEVELOPED WORLD

But juniper's greatest value has always been in its medicinal properties, where it has been held in high regard by medicine men and women for as long as medicine has been documented.

The Zuni of New Mexico would burn twigs of juniper then infuse them in hot water, making a kind of tea that was administered as a relaxant to pregnant women during labour. The Canadian Cree made a tea from the root of the plant, while the Micmac and Malachite tribes (also of Canada) used juniper for sprains, wounds, tuberculosis, ulcers and rheumatism. The Shoshone boiled a tea from the berries and used it to treat kidney and bladder infections.

The Guna People, who occupy the San Blas Islands off the east coast of Panama, would smear ground-up juniper berries all over their bodies to fend off parasitic cat fish that would attack them when they went swimming, ironically, to catch fish.

In traditional Chinese medicine juniper is prescribed to tackle urinary infections and indeed any discomfort or disease centred around the lower or middle abdominal region. In central European folk medicine the oil extracted from the berries was regarded as a cure-all for typhoid, cholera, dysentery, tapeworms and various other afflictions you might associate with the poverty-stricken.

In Medieval times juniper berries were ground down and used as an antibacterial salve, which would be applied to cuts and wounds. For infections of the mouth you might be instructed to chew on juniper berries for a day to ward off microbial infection.

Juniper's more esoteric uses include its capability of driving off evil spirits. Icelandic and Nordic tribes would wear sprigs of juniper about their person to protect the bearer from wild animal attacks. Wreaths made from juniper sprigs might also have hung above your door in efforts to protect the household from bad luck. All good shamans should turn to juniper when needing to cleanse or purify an area and drive away misfortune. Burning the leaves, roots, berries or twigs was common amongst Druids too. The Celts had similar ideas, fumigating the sick or possessed with juniper smoke until the subject recovered or died.

The Romans kept some in the their medicine cabinets, too. In the 2nd Century AD the Greco-Roman physician Galen noted that juniper berries 'cleanse the liver and kidneys, and they evidently thin any thick and viscous juices, and for this reason they are mixed in health medicines.' Galen had probably ascertained this from Pliny

Juniperus Sabina

MARCVS CATO CLAR. OLYM

ABOVE Juniper is one of mankind's oldest medicines. Alcohol is another…

ABOVE Cato the Elder is often considered to be the first Roman to have written in Latin. He was an avid juniper grower, too.

INDIAN ALTAR AND RUINS OF OLD ZUNI

ABOVE Juniper burgers were common in some native North American communities.

the Elder whose enormous 37-book *Naturalis Historia*, which is one of the largest pieces of work to have survived the Roman Empire, included an entire volume dedicated to botany, wine and medicine. Pliny mentions juniper 22 times in *Naturalis Historia*, celebrating the fruit's effectiveness at dispelling flatulence and stopping coughs, as well as its effectiveness as a diuretic.

Pliny also makes reference to Cato the Elder for juniper-based know-how. Cato (b. 234 BC) was the consummate Roman statesman, an accomplished soldier, as well as a farmer who did a good job at playing doctor to his family and veterinarian to his livestock. If we're to believe Cato, a vineyard was the best sort of agricultural estate to possess, but even better if you can use that wine to make medicine. He lists a lot of botanical recipes in his book *De Agri Cultura* 'On Agriculture' (c. 160 BC) mostly derived from his garden such as hellebore and myrtle; one recipe, however, is for a wine-based juniper infusion used to cure gout and urinary infections. Cato lived to the ripe old age of 85, an achievement that many attribute to his fondness for his self-prescribed farm tonics.

The oldest reference to juniper's use as a medicine takes us back almost 4,000 years, to Ancient Egypt. A number of important medical scrolls were written between 1800-1500 BC, including the Eber Papyrus and the Kahun Papyrus, the latter of which is the earliest known medical text in existence. Many of these treatments relied on a healthy measure of magic, chanting, or some very unusual ingredients (e.g. cat's fat), so suffice to say that they are not all as firmly rooted in scientific principle as each other. Juniper was used to treat digestive ailments, soothe chest pains and ease stomach cramps. The Eber Papyrus lists a recipe used to treat tapeworms that calls for 'juniper berries five parts, white oil five parts, taken for one day.'

THE SPICE TRADE AND THE ORIGINS OF JUNIPER SPIRITS

When the distillation of wine was first discovered by European alchemists, the fiery, volatile liquid that emanated from the alembic still was dubbed *aqua vitae* (water of life). It was genuinely believed by Arnaldus de Villa Nova, a 13th-century professor from the University of Montpellier and the godfather of medical chemistry, to be a cure for mortality: 'We call it *aqua vitae*, and this name is remarkably suitable, since it really is the water of immortality. It prolongs life, clears away ill-humours, strengthens the heart, and maintains youth.'

The knowledge of distillation steadily disseminated through Europe, via monasteries and new-fangled universities, evolving into regional variants, made from barley, grapes, rye and wheat. Over the coming centuries these distillates would graduate into the spirit categories of whisky, brandy and vodka that we recognize today.

At some point, probably during the early 13th century, *aqua vitae* arrived in the Low Countries, an area comprising 17 individual states

LEFT This 1506 engraving depicts the alchemist and astrologer Arnaldus de Villa Nova picking grapes for wine.

covering modern-day Holland, Belgium, Luxembourg, and parts of France and Germany. At that time the Low Countries were enjoying a prosperous period. Towns were designed and built from scratch, rather than being bodged together from existing settlements. Canals and waterways provided a broad and efficient trade network for goods and materials. The city of Antwerp, in its centre, was fast becoming a spiritual and intellectual hub, and by the middle of the 1400s, it was the richest city in Europe.

The population swelled as a result and it didn't take long for physicians, chemists and Cistercian monks to begin documenting the newest and trendiest findings in the world of science and alchemy. One of the earliest of these comes from *Der Naturen Bloeme* by Jacob van Maerlant. Published in 1269. This work was a translation of a slightly earlier volume of books titled *Opus de Natura Rerum* (A Collection of Natural Occurrences) – by a theologian called Thomas de Cantimpré, who was born in 1201.

Spread over 20 volumes, and written entirely in rhyme, it took de Cantimpré 15 years to write what was, at the time, probably the most exhaustive text on natural history in existence. An entire volume of the text is dedicated to medicinal plants and their various uses, and included within that is provision for boiled rainwater or wine containing juniper berries, used to treat stomach pain.

By the end of the 14th century, juniper wines and spirits were stocked in the medical cabinets of any physician worth their salt. A 1578 translation of Rembert Dodoens' *A Nievve Herbal* (A History of Plants) celebrates the juniper berry's properties as 'good for the stomacke, lunges, liver and kidneys: it cureth the olde cough, the "gripinges" and "windinesse of the belly", and "provoketh brine"'. The passage finishes with instructions, 'to be boiled in wine or honied water and dronken'. Thanks to books like *Constelijck Distilleerboet*, by Phillip Hermanni, an Antwerp-based physician, the knowledge required to make these spirits was in the public domain. Hermanni's 'distillation for doctors' handbook included a recipe for *geneverbessenwater* (juniper berry water) that saw the berries crushed, sprinkled with wine, and distilled in an alembic pot still. Hermanni goes on to describe how the liquid can be used for digestive disorders, colds, plague and to treat bites from venomous animals.

The 14th century also saw the first murmurings of a very important and necessary (for the purposes of this book) shift in the way that spirits were perceived and consumed. The first example of this in the Low Countries (where we would soon see the birth of genever) comes from a manuscript written by Flemish alchemist Johannes van Aalter, in 1351. The text was copied from an earlier piece, the author unknown, but the lucid appraisal of alcohol's social effects is quite uncanny: 'It makes people forget human sorrow and makes the heart glad and strong and courageous.'

BELOW Aided by good town planning, Antwerp was Europe's most prosperous city in the 15th century.

For a well-motivated 15th-century alcoholic, spirits would soon become a quick and easy route to inebriation. By flavouring these *aqua vitae*, one could mask some of that rough-hewn temperament, offering a delicious in-road into botanical spirits. The fact that many of these so-called botanicals were also endowed with impressive medicinal benefits was just an added bonus. A change was clearly afoot and all the cogs were beginning to align.

ABOVE The complex process of distillation as depicted in the 1519 book, *Liber de Arte Distillandi, Simplicia et Composita*.

The only problem now was that many of these fruits and spices were still quite expensive. Nutmeg, for example, was worth more than its weight in gold, and many of these products could only get to you via the complex spice trade routes that ran through the Middle East into Europe via Constantinople and Venice. When the Ottoman Empire took control of Constantinople in 1453, they imposed huge levies on spices that passed through the city. It was demand for these spices (ginger, cassia, cardamom and pepper) that triggered the age of discovery, as European nations were forced to find new routes over sea to the sources of these commodities. They were incredibly expensive for an average European to purchase however, and any access outside of medical circles was rare and really only the preserve of the rich and powerful, which is what makes the next part of the story so incredible.

THE BIRTH OF GENEVER

In 1495 a wealthy merchant from a region known as the Duchy of Guelders (now a part of The Netherlands, near Arnhem) decided it would be a good idea to have a book written for him. Being a household guide, the book documented some of the lavish recipes he and his family were enjoying at the time. Included was a brandy recipe made from '10 quarts of wine thinned with clear hamburg beer.' After distillation the liquid would be redistilled with 'two handfuls of dried sage, 1lb of cloves, 12 whole nutmegs, cardamom, cinnamon, galangal, ginger, grains of paradise' and – crucially – 'juniper berries.' The spices were placed in a cloth sack and suspended above the distillate, allowing the vapours to extract their flavour. Grinding diamonds over white truffle is as close a comparison as I can imagine to expressing the extravagance of such a recipe during that period. It's for this reason that it's highly unlikely that the drink was intended for anything other than sinful pleasures.

BELOW This reproduction of a copper engraving shows the sack of Antwerp by Spanish forces on 4th November 1576.

This was the dawn of a new era of spirits, where recreational delight superseded medicinal comfort. Juniper was cheap, readily available and tasty. It quickly assumed its modern role and became the poster-boy for the flavoured spirits movement.

LAWS & WARS

The early 16th century saw consecutively poor grape harvests in the Low Countries that lasted over two decades. The price of wine went up, so distillers turned to beer instead. The fermented grain mash of rye and malted barley quickly became known as *moutwijn* (malt wine) and its distillate, *korenbrandewijn* (grain burnt wine), which was later shortened down to *korenwijn* – a term that is useful to know when navigating genever styles. In English it's a common mistake to associate *korenwijn* with corn, but it can in fact be made from any cereal, and would not have been made with corn until at least the 1880s.

Any flavoured spirit made from flavoured *korenwijn* would adopt the name of its chief ingredient to avoid any confusion as to what it was. It's not known who first used the term genever (the French word for juniper) or if indeed anyone prior to 1495 had experimented with it. The van Dale dictionary, The Netherlands' equivalent of the Oxford English Dictionary, first listed the word (in reference to the drink) in 1672, but production of juniper spirits in Holland and Belgium had already been galvanized some 100 years prior to that.

The 16th century was a tumultuous time for the Low Countries. The year 1568 marked the beginning of what would later be known as the Eighty Years' War. In the briefest of summaries, the war was a Protestant uprising centred around the Low Countries and aimed at their then sovereign ruler, Spain. During the considerable period of the war, the city of Antwerp was eviscerated of its populous, as panic-stricken residents fled to the north, to France, to neighbouring German cities, or to the safer towns of Hasselt and Weesp. Some 6,000 Flemish Protestants had fled to London by 1570, paving the way for the genever/gin boom that followed later. The fall of Antwerp in 1585 is seen by many as the turning point in relations between the northern and southern Low Countries, drawing a line in the sand between the areas that would one day form the Netherlands and Belgium.

Consistent with most wars of the era, next, inevitably, came a ban on distilling from fruit or cereal, imposed in 1601 by a government dealing with a very apparent national food shortage. The ban wouldn't be lifted until 1713, a full 112 years later. But the dictate was not recognized in the north, so for a down-on-his-luck distiller the northern towns posed a tempting prospect. As the south was torn apart, the new Dutch Republic in the north accepted swarms of skilled refugees from Antwerp, laying down the foundations of the 'Dutch Golden Age'.

EMERGENCE OF AN INDUSTRY

Many fresh-off-the-cart brewers and distillers gravitated towards Schiedam, a neighbouring city to Rotterdam, and a place whose name would become synonymous with spirits production over the next 200 years. Included amongst the folk on the move was a Flemish family by the name of Bols (meaning 'arrow'), who fled to Cologne initially, then eventually settled just outside of Amsterdam in 1575. They set up a distillery called 't Lootsje ('the little shed') and began making spiced spirits and liqueurs. Later, in 1664, they added genever to their portfolio. Bols is now the oldest spirits brand in the world.

Amsterdam gratefully took on the mantle of Europe's premier trading port and in 1602 the Dutch East Indies Company (VOC) was founded. More a roving nation than a business, the VOC would soon become the biggest company in the world, and with over 30,000 employees spread across the globe, the world's first multi-national corporation. The VOC traded in everything: spices, precious metals, tea, coffee, cotton, textiles and sugar. It also minted its own currency, waged wars, imprisoned slaves and established colonies. It turned Holland into a 17th-century super-power. Genever travelled to all the four corners of the world and was used for trading, or just

RIGHT Genever advertising during the boom times was often garish, rarely subtle, and usually fun.

BELOW The Dutch first arrived in Indonesia in 1596 and six years later established the Dutch East India Company to exploit the lucrative spice trade.

to provide a familiar taste of home. Most Dutch sailors were entitled to between 150-200 ml (5–7 fl. oz.) of genever every day. In the colonies it was popular too, where residents would down *soopjes* (shots) of colloquially named proto-cocktails, like *papegaaiensoep* (parrot soup), *hap snert* (bite of pea soup) and *dikop* (fat head).

Spirits were stored by the barrel back then, meaning that all of the spirits distributed abroad, and most of those drunk at home, would have undergone some degree of barrel ageing. This would place them closer in style to a light whisky than a modern-day gin.

With the trade network established, genever production in Holland boomed. Schiedam had 37 distilleries at the beginning of the 17th century, but it was more like 250 by the turn of the next. By the 1880s, there would be nearly 400 and the industry was employing over three-quarters of the city's 6,000 residents in milling, malting, brewing, distilling and barrelling. Twenty enormous windmills were the backbone of the Schiedam spirits machine, grinding the huge volumes of cereal that entered the city, piled high on Dutch flute boats that navigated along the gridlocked river Nieuwe Maas. The tallest and widest windmills in the world were all in Schiedam at that time (a fact that remains to this day) grossly mis-proportioned in their efforts to capture their share of the city's breeze.

But the slick sheen of a well-oiled industry also concealed a grave defilement of the city and its people. The coal-field distilleries polluted the air and dyed the city black – awarding Schiedam its label as the 'Black Nazareth' – and off-spill from the still's condensers poisoned the water. And what with all that booze, alcoholism ensued, perpetuated by the squalid living conditions and low pay received by the distillery workers. Schiedam became a sprawling workhouse of industry, bolstered by a new global demand for genever. Five original windmills can still be seen in Schiedam today. They are the five largest windmills in the world (the biggest, De Noord, is 33.3 m (110 ft) high) and have recently been joined by a sixth windmill that was rebuilt in 2011 on the site of an original 1715 mill.

The fable of Dr. Sylvius

Franciscus Sylvius de la Boe was a professor of medicine at Leiden University, Holland, between 1658 and 1672. During his time at the University, Sylvius cooked up no small quantity of juniper-based tonics, and prior to that he had worked as a plague doctor, where juniper had no doubt featured in his arsenal of preventive remedies. It's fair to say that Dr. Sylvius is historically one of juniper's most reliable advocates. Nowadays, however, he is widely and erroneously credited as the man who invented genever.

There are plenty of reasons why Sylvius couldn't possibly have been the inventor of genever, or juniper spirits. The previous pages of this very book can attest to the preliminary work of such things having taken place years before Sylvius appeared on the scene. The fact that Sylvius was only born in 1614 – late enough to have entirely missed the Flemmish spirits boom of the 16th century – should be proof enough, but just to be sure, it's worth pointing out genever was never mentioned in any of his surviving research, nor was he ever cited more than once regarding his distilling expertise. Oh, and did I mention he was German, born in Hanover?

Case closed.

THE FASHIONABLE
LONDON DRINK

The Dutch-born William of Orange (William III) arrived in
England in 1688. His seizure of crown was a surprisingly peaceful
affair in an otherwise bloody period of history – in fact, Parliament
more or less propped the door open for him. The man he ousted,
James II, the last Roman Catholic monarch to reign over the
Kingdoms, was very much in the dog house as far as popular
opinion went. Dethroned and desolate, James skulked off to
Catholic France, and all things French became deeply uncool.

William's first act as King was to declare war on France, which
included banning the import of French brandy outright. William
also lowered taxes on cereals, earning him a big 'thumbs-up'
from the landed gentry who owned most of the countryside,
and loosened up the laws concerning distilling to encourage
more people to buy home-grown grains. It was a wicked cocktail
of policies and the result, as with any good cocktail, was one of
total inebriation.

It's for the reasons above, along with William's Dutch origins, that
he is often credited as the man responsible for making genever
(and gin) fashionable in England. William's relaxing of the rules
meant that more or less anyone could bag themselves a distilling
licence with nothing more than an administration fee and a waiting
period of ten days to see if anyone objected. Of course 'King Billy'
(as he was known to the Scots) never intended the outright anarchy
that ensued (he wouldn't live to see the worst of it) and to some
extent he achieved what he set out to, but in the process condemned
London to sixty years of drunken carnage.

But gin, or as it was still known then, genever, was already reasonably well established in London before William came along; in fact it was doing quite alright before William's father was born, too. Distillation was not as widespread in England as other European countries like the Low Countries, but had long been the preserve of curious monks and crackpot alchemists as far back as the 14th century. Henry VIII's dissolution of the monasteries in 1534 forced great numbers of the well-informed monks from the sanctuary of their chapels out into the badlands of civilisation.

ABOVE London's lust for gin was in place before William III's accession. But his policies lit the fuse that ignited the gin explosion.

Many of these learned men developed trades in activities consistent with their previous monastic practices: carpentry, weaving textiles, baking bread, brewing beer and distilling spirits. One hundred years after Henry VIII founded the Church of England, there were over 200 distilleries in London.

It was during the Eighty Years' War (1568–1648) that juniper spirits would have first appeared in London taverns. In December 1585, Elizabeth I sent 6000 armed men to the Low Countries to provide support against Spanish forces. They failed to suppress the Fall of Antwerp, but during their time travelling and fighting alongside their Dutch comrades the English noticed the Dutch men partook in a certain strange ritual. This took the form of small bottles on

ABOVE This etching shows spirit drinking and pipe smoking in 17th-century Holland. The liquor wasn't to everyone's tastes, as the chap on the right would attest to.

their belts, like hip flasks, which they would customarily swig back before wading into the battle. The English observed the courage exhibited by their Dutch compatriots, later coining the term 'Dutch Courage'. It wouldn't be the last time that the Dutch and English fought side by side. During the Thirty Years' War (1618–1648), which was one of the bloodiest and nastiest in European history, the English and Dutch troops once again fought alongside each other in opposition to Spain and the Holy Roman Empire. On that occasion it's quite likely that both the English and the Dutch were knocking back bottles of 'courage'.

As is consistent with other parts of Europe, juniper spirits were also a favourite of English doctors and physicians. Gervase Markham's 1615 guide to household management, *The English Housewife*, included a recipe for eyedrops that featured juniper, fennel and gromwell seeds. London's pre-eminent 17th-century chronicler, Samuel Pepys, wrote in 1663 that he had been advised by a friend to take 'strong water made from juniper' to cure a severe case of constipation.

But one of the earliest and perhaps improbable sources of early juniper spirits in England eminated not from the physicians table, but the kitchen table. Sir Hugh Plat (inventor and sometime hero of the housewife) published *Delightes For Ladies*, in 1602, which included a whole section dedicated to recipes for distilling in the home. One recipe, for a drink called 'Spirits of Spices', calls for 'cloves, mace, nutmegs, juniper, rosemary' in no specific quantities. This was mixed with 'strong and sweet water' then distilled over a bain marie or hot ashes. The result? According to Plat you can hope for a 'delicate spirit of each of the said aromatical bodies.' If we resist being too critical of the recipe, Plat's 'Spirits of Spices' could be regarded as England's first proto-gin.

GIN AT THE TURN OF THE 18TH CENTURY

While the likes of Plat and Markham served a purpose, at least as far as the enterprising housewife was concerned, England was in dire need of some practical instruction relating to the art of distillation. It arrived (almost exactly as requested) in 1692, in the form of *The Whole Art of Distillation Practically Stated*, by William Y-Worth. Y-Worth, an immigrant from Holland, made no bones about it: his was the only credible work concerning distillation available. Sadly, only one recipe in the entire book uses juniper, and the spirit is intended for medicinal purposes.

Following Y-Worth's book, *The Distiller of London* by Thomas Cademan was published in 1698. This distilling manual was actually a private handbook for London's Worshipful Company of Distillers. As a Livery Company of the City of London, this group was founded in 1638 to oversee and regulate the production of spirits in London. Caveman's book is an important one, because it lists a number of recipes (by number rather than name) which include juniper, and some where juniper is the chief ingredient. The recipes are often extravagant, incorporating expensive imported spices (such as nutmeg and cloves), dried citrus peels and fresh berries. They were labour-intensive too, but the eventual outcome would have been a product of exceptional quality for the period.

As the gin craze began to kick hard (page 38) things began to turn sour. The books that followed approached the subject of juniper and genever more cautiously. Ambrose Cooper's *The Compleat Practical Distiller* (1757) includes a simple recipe for gin that calls for 'three pounds of juniper berries, proof spirit ten gallons, water four gallons' which is distilled in the classic way.

The law meant it was cheap and easy to buy alcohol, and not difficult to produce some imitation genever. A lack of distilling expertise lead to the gin makers casually disregarding Dutch genever practices (including the all-important malt wine) and focus on infusing poorly-made neutral alcohol with botanicals, the latter to mask the impure and unpleasant flavour of the neutral spirits. Gin became as cheap as beer, but packed a much bigger punch. In time, the botanicals too would be considered an unnecessary expense.

In Cooper's book he also informs the reader that the 'common sort of gins' are made using oil of turpentine, a compound extracted from pine tree resin that bears some resemblance to the piney aroma of juniper. He seems more confused than disgusted by the this practice, adding that 'it is surprising that people should accustom themselves to drinking it for pleasure.'

'Common Gin' or 'Gineva' production was a two- part process in your average slum setup. No-one distilled their own spirit from scratch, so it first had to be bought in from a larger distillery. These distilleries would take beer and run it through pot stills a couple of times to make 'proof spirit'. This was a time before the continuous still had been invented, so the proof spirit would not be entirely neutral in its character, but quite likely entirely awful. A large chunk of this proof spirit came from Scotland, where the game was to run your still as fast as possible, heedless of any negative effects it might have to the taste or safety of your spirit.

Once the proof spirit arrived at your door, all that was left was to flavour it. The gentry were all drinking imported genever, so the smart move would have been to hash together some pseudo-genever of your own. Unfortunately botanicals were seen as time-wasting and expensive. Far better to compound salts, acids and toxic extracts into your product, right? One gin recipe from the 1740s, from the firm of Beaufoy, James and Co., doesn't even mention juniper: 'Oil of vitriol, oil of almonds, oil of turpentine, spirits of wine, lamp sugar, lime water, rose water, alum, salt of tartar.'

It was gin that fuelled the gin craze, but in its guise as inexpensive fire water, consumed without restraint. Not the aromatically balanced botanical spirit that we recognize gin as today.

It might have tasted bad, but that didn't stop tenacious types knocking it back. But not everyone swigged straight from the flagon. Mixing gin with sweet cordials, like peppermint or lovage, took the edge off and made a kind of pseudo-liqueur. Another one of the more popular ways of drinking gin was with a side helping of gingerbread. Ginger really was the flavour of London in the early 18th century (along with gin, of course) largely thanks to colonies in India and the Caribbean doing a damn fine job of growing the stuff. This made ginger comparatively cheap compared to other spices and stalls selling fermented ginger beer lined many of the traditional market streets of London, like Petticoat Lane. In 1740 Joseph Stone, a prominent spice merchant based on High Holborn, loaned his name to the Finsbury Distillery Company, and Stone's Green Ginger Wine was born. But it was perhaps in the form of gingerbread, coupled with a measure of warm gin, that ginger truly excelled itself. When the Thames froze over and there was little else to do, other than spectate over executions and get drunk, it was gin and spiced gingerbread that filled a Londoner's belly.

THE BROKEN PROMISE

Britain's grand conquests abroad made London an enticing prospect for starry-eyed immigrants. But on their arrival into London's docks, reality would have hit quite hard. Those who brought a trade with them stood some small chance of a normal, honest existence. Those who didn't found themselves forcefully strained through convoluted layers of bedlam and poverty, coming to rest, broken and dejected, only once they reached the guts of one of London's inner-city slums. And it would be in the slums that 'gin' would rally its forces. It would be the sympathizer to the impoverished, and would lead to ruin for all of those who went near it.

ABOVE When the River Thames froze over in 1814, you can bet that Londoners turned to gin and gingerbread to warm themselves up.

RIGHT An 18th-century gingerbread seller displays his wares on the streets of Mayfair.

THE GIN CRAZE

The word 'gin' didn't appear in the Oxford English Dictionary until 1714. Defined as 'an infamous liquor' it had clearly made its mark already. During the early days of the 'craze' gin was known as geneva or 'Madame Geneva'. Probably no coincidence that gin's entry in to the dictionary coincided with Bernard Mandeville's 'Fable of the Bees', a poem that was published in 1705, followed by a book, which first appeared in 1714.

In his frank and detailed description of London's various vices and corruptions, Mandeville gives us one of the earliest insights into gin as a purely ruinous force, as well as one of the earliest uses of the word 'gin'. 'Nothing is more destructive, either in regard to the Health or the Vigilance and Industry of the Poor than the infamous Liquor, the name of which, deriv'd from Junipera in Dutch, is now by frequent use and the laconic spirit of the nation, from a word of middling length shrunk into a monosyllable, intoxicating GIN'.

Slowly at first but gathering pace, the overconsumption of gin became endemic. Far removed from the blithe alcoholism associated with beer and wine, it was perceived by those lucky enough to escape its clutches as perfectly abhorrent. Gin was the widespread social drug of the time that preyed on the poor and vulnerable, gutting London from the inside out. Dr Stephen Hales, an anti-gin campaigner, wrote in 1734 that 'Man, has unhappily found means to extract, from what God intended for his refreshment, a most pernicious and intoxicating liquor.' In the 1730s around five million gallons of raw spirits were being distilled in London every year, and less than 10% of it would ever leave the city.

The population of London as a whole was relatively stagnant between 1725 and 1750, but this was only due to the steady influx of migrants. The death rate in London during the mid-1700s exceeded the birth rate. In the worst areas, a newborn had less than an 80% chance of making it to the age of two. Many families were forced to live in single rooms in ramshackle tenements or in damp cellars, with no sanitation or fresh air. Drinking water was often contaminated by raw sewage and garbage was left rotting in the street. Problems with the disposal of the dead often added to the stench and decay. Many London graveyards became full to capacity, and coffins were sometimes left partially uncovered in 'poor holes' close to local houses and businesses. It's little wonder that the poor turned to gin as a release from the hardships of survival.

Imagine every single newsagent, store, supermarket and street vendor in central London turning their hand to selling gin. Then imagine that it's cheaper than bread or milk and that anyone can buy it: violent drunks, the elderly and infirm, children. Finally, imagine that it's not only highly addictive, but poisonous, laced with added 'flavour-enhancing' properties that when consumed in large quantities cause blindness, death or the loss of one's mind.

It's easy to imagine widespread turmoil throughout the entire city, but 'dramming' was really only centred around the poorest districts. In 1700 London had a population of 575,000, which made it the largest metropolis in Europe. While the residents of St. Giles in the Fields, an area near Charing Cross Road, got drunk for (literally) a penny, the city could press on with business as usual, preoccupied and only vaguely aware of the horrors taking place around the corner. Gentleman, politicians, merchants and scholars wouldn't venture into the fleshpots of Holborn or Shoreditch. They would meet in nearby Cornhill to drink coffee and discuss politics, trade, the colonies, science or poetry. Perhaps some might have indulged in a glass of gin on occasion, but it would be imported Holland's Gin, not the ghastly stuff produced in some squalid basement. The single biggest reason that the gin craze lasted so long and its effects were so brutal is the ignorance of the upper classes to what was taking place under their noses.

If the gin craze was a storm, then the area of St. Giles in the Fields was the centre of the deluge. Renowned as one of the country's biggest slums, for the 20,000 people living there gin was a simple, cheap and accessible solution to all of their problems.

As you might expect, there is no shortage of harrowing stories from the period. As a researcher, it becomes a macabre process of selection, sifting through the fallout and singling out the accounts that best represent the grim horror of the gin craze. William Hogarth's 'Gin Lane'

ABOVE While the poor got drunk on gin in the 18th century, the upper classes drank coffee and discussed politics.

etching might seem like a grizzly exaggeration of events, but the true plight of the people embroiled in the gin craze was perhaps even worse than his famous depiction (page 42).

One of the most disturbing and notorious tales from the period is of Judith Dufour. In 1734 Dufour deposited her unclothed two-year-old daughter, Mary, at the workhouse where she was employed, then returned the following day to claim her. Now fully clothed, she stripped the child of her clothes, then strangled her to death, dumped her body in a ditch. She then sold the clothes for 1 shilling and 4 pence and used her earnings to buy gin.

Spare a thought, too, for Joseph Barret – a 42-year-old labourer, who was hanged in 1728 for beating his son to death. Barret's final confession is a harrowing account of how his son (James) spent his days begging for money and his nights 'drinking until he appeared worse than a beast, quite out of his senses.' Barret apparently had 'no evil intention' and planned only to 'reclaim [James] from his wild courses.' Barret's punishment was too savage however, and James died in his bed. He was eleven years old.

By 1751 half of all the British wheat harvest was used to make spirits. There were reportedly 17,000 'private gin shops' in London and almost half of them were in Holborn. That's approximately one shop for every black cab in Greater London today. And that figure only represents the gin specialists! It doesn't include all the taverns and public houses that also sold gin by the bucket load. Neither does it include the street markets, grocers, chandlers, barbers, barrows and brothels that also did a roaring trade.

Some estimates – and they can really only be estimates – suggest that over 10 million gallons of gin were consumed in London that year. A worthy effort for a population of only 700,000, helped along by the fact that many factory workers were partly paid in gin. Follow the maths down and you're looking at a pint of gin per week for every single London citizen. The novelist Henry Fielding argued that there would soon be 'few of the common people left to drink it' if the situation continued.

ABOVE The 'Rookery' in St. Giles, in Bloomsbury, London, where the gin flowed like water and where both water and gin were liable to poison you.

GIN LANE

Poets, playwrights and journalists turned their attention to the scourge, publicly voicing their concerns over the parasite that was gnawing at London's underbelly. It was in 1751 that William Hogarth unveiled his remarkable 'Gin Lane' etching. Burdened with ghastly imagery, the scene was designed to shock all who laid eyes on it, serving as a morbid checklist of gin's capacity to induce social decay, drunkenness, starvation, depression, violence, suicide, infanticide and madness.

The motives behind Gin Lane are a little more convoluted than the simple intentions of a respected artist performing a much needed public service. The Treaty of Aix-la-Chapelle of 1748 marked the end of the War of the Austrian Sucession, the upshot of which would see the return of around 80,000 soldiers who had been fighting abroad. That's a lot of soldiers to feed and water, and knowing the ease with which fighting men could be drawn into Madame Geneva's embrace, public tensions were strung tight. Hogarth produced Gin Lane and the sister piece, Beer Street, in response to the public's demand for another Gin Act (pages 44–47). There have been suggestions that Hogarth was in cahoots with the brewers, and that the pieces were pure propaganda, diverting the masses away from their demon water, and promoting the drinking of good, clean, honest beer. Either way, Gin Lane is the most prominent piece of satire to emerge from the gin craze, and one of the more effective weapons in gin's undoing.

Gin Lane is certainly worthy of a few minutes' close inspection, where the most observant amongst you will find countless sub-plots in the wider story of gin's destructive force. In the foreground we are naturally drawn to the image of the inebriated mother, cheerfully oblivious to the fact that she has dropped her child in favour of a snuff box. In front of her sits a skeletal man, clutching

a flagon of gin and a ballad entitled 'The Downfall of Madam Gin'
– its objective plainly fallen by the wayside. Behind and to the right
an elderly woman is fed gin from her position in a barrow and
a pair of St Giles orphans share a dram while people riot outside
a gin distillery. The pawnbroker on the left of the scene is doing
a roaring trade as the three-sphered sign doubles up as a cross
above the distant Bloomsbury church spire. The message is clear:
the people of Gin Lane have placed their faith in an altogether
different kind of spirit. The middle distance is a picture of more
tumultuous behaviour: dilapidation, death, and a man beating
himself over the head with a pair of bellows while holding aloft
a dead child on a spike. The detail of the composition even stretches
to the silhouetted figures of a funeral procession working their way
through the rubble at the far end of Gin Lane.

RIGHT The
illustrations of George
Cruikshank vilified the
gin shops for their
role in the moral and
physical decay of the
lower classes.

THE GIN ACTS

In the 1720s, the government finally took notice of the effect that London gin was having on its poorest inhabitants declaring that 'the drinking of spirits is... very common among the people of inferior rank and the constant and excessive use thereof tends greatly to the destruction of their healths, enervating them, and rendering them unfit for useful labour and service.'

The first of six Gin Acts, spread across a 30-year period, was made law in 1729, in the wake of the doubling of the spirit's production in the previous 10 years. The purpose of the First Act was to curb the manufacture and consumption of gin by imposing a higher tax of five shillings per gallon on 'compound waters'. The price of a retail licence also went up to £20 (US$30), around £1,800 (US$2,670) in today's money. Targeting the troublesome compounders should have been a good tactic, but the Act failed to deal with the two dozen-or-so distillers who were the ones making the spirit in the first place. It didn't work. Consumption continued to rise and taxes were left unpaid.

LEFT In this 1829 etching by George Cruikshank, gin shop patrons don't realize that ruin, poverty and death surround them.

The Second Act, in 1733, did away with the extra duty on 'compound waters' and banned the sale of gin in the street altogether. If you were caught, a £10 (US$15) fine would be imposed, and if you assisted in a conviction a £5 (US$7.50) reward would be granted.

This was quickly followed by the Third Act, in 1736, which raised the fine for unlicensed retailers to £100 (US$150) and the fine for street-selling to £10 (US$15). The price of a licence more than doubled, to an exorbitant £50 (US$75), and a 20 shilling per gallon tax was applied to gin sold in small quantities. The cost was so extreme that it should have crippled compounding altogether. But only two applications for licences were ever filed. The trick now was not to get caught. Around 4,000 rewards were claimed over the next two years, but known informants were beaten bloody in the streets or thrown into the River Thames. One poor man was 'set upon an ass' and paraded down Bond Street while having stones and mud thrown at him.

Enterprising gin sellers developed new and elaborate methods to inconspicuously deliver their payloads to wanting customers. The best example of this is the 'Puss and Mew' contraption, pioneered by Dudley Bradstreet. These human-operated gin vending machines were denoted by a wooden carving of a cat on a wall. Those in need of a fix would approach the cat and whisper 'puss'. If anyone was listening, and gin was available (which it surely was) the response would come back 'Mew', to which the patron would place a penny in a drawer and gin would be dispensed out of lead pipe protruding out of the wall.

Soon, though, the number of people flouting the law was so tremendous that the time for discretion had passed. The Gin Act of 1743 took a different tack altogether. Duty on spirits was raised, but the cost of a licence was slashed to £1 (US$1.50) and the duty on compounded spirits was cut to a fraction of its previous rate. Anti-gin campaigners saw this as surrendering to popular demand but it had the desired effect, with thousands of licences issued over the following years. But this was not just about finding salvation for the lower class, the tax revenue was desperately needed to fund the war effort overseas.

As the courtier Lord Hervey put it, 'This Bill is an experiment of a very daring kind... to find out how far the vices of the population may be made useful to the government [and] what taxes may be raised upon poison.'

BELOW A satirical funeral procession for Madame Geneva. But was she really dead?

The Gin Act of 1747 became the undoing of the previous one however, as the ever-powerful distillers revolted and were granted £5 (US$7.50) licences and the opportunity to sell direct from shops. The effect was clear to see as, in 1750, gin consumption was nearing an all-time high.

Finally, the Gin Act of 1751 was introduced and this successfully tackled all the issues contributing to mass consumption. Distillers were banned from selling gin in shops, and workhouses and prisons were banned from distributing gin amongst their residents. Licence fees were doubled and were only granted to public houses. Perhaps the most effective blow was the withdrawal of rights to the distillers concerning debt collection. The distillers had, until then, had the full force of the law behind them when it came to unpaid invoices from compounders. This Act stated that debts of less than £1 (US$1.50) could no longer be legally recovered, so the prospect of dealing with these small-time operations, whose credit barely stretched beyond a few shillings, became quite unappealing.

There is not in nature so unhealthy a liquor as Geneva, especially as commonly sold; it curdles the blood, stupefies the senses, it weakens the nerves it spoils the eyesights, and entirely ruins the stomach.

Daniel Defoe, 1928

THE GENTLEMEN
OF GIN

The 1751 Gin Act suppressed the public appetite for gin by keeping
check of the compounders' production capabilities. That alone might
have been enough to keep Madame Geneva down, but disastrous
grain harvests in 1757 meant that she wouldn't be getting back any
time soon. As corn was held back for more important things (like
food), its use in distilling was outlawed from 1757 through to 1760.
That didn't stop distillers importing molasses, but the trickle of
liquor was a fraction of what it had been. By 1761 gin consumption
in London was down to less than 20% of the level it had been ten
years previously, at around 2 million gallons. By that time most of
the small distillers and compounders with their limited buying
power had already been squeezed out of the marketplace. The price
of gin went up in reflection of the elevated production cost and the
relative scarcity. Gradually the lower classes turned their attention

BELOW By 1900, the Gilbey's Distillery in London
covered over 8 hectares (20 acres) of land.

to relative safety of beer and porter. The whole point of gin had been that it was cheap, but it wasn't cheap anymore. Now, if the gin category were to survive at all, the quality would have to go up.

Fortunately, Britain was on the cusp of the industrial revolution and it was time for gin to go industrial too. Emerging from the ruin of the gin craze, the first families of gin would establish themselves during this era. A name, rather than a brand, flagons of Booth's and Gordon's spoke of reliability and accountability in a marketplace that had been previously full to the brim with anonymity.

Clerkenwell would soon become ground zero in London's next explosive phase of gin production. Named after the Clerk's Well (but also featuring the Skinner's Well and Sadler's Well), this area had been known since medieval times as the best source of clean water in all of London. It's for this reason that some of London's biggest breweries had already set up shop there. The Clerkenwell and Goswell Road areas proved popular with the distillers and rectifiers of the day.

One of the earliest purpose-built distilleries was John & William Nicholson & Co, who started making gin there in 1736, on St. John Street. Later, they acquired another distillery in Mile End and began producing their Lamplighter Gin, a product that would remain popular right up until the 1970s.

Langdale's on London's Holborn Hill was established in 1745. Langdale's Gin became extremely popular in London over the next few decades, although it was often diluted by bootleg sellers. Sadly the distillery was gutted on the sixth day of the anti-Catholic Gordon Riots of 1780.

The Booth family, who were established wine merchants as far back as the 16th century, added distilling to their repertoire in 1740. They built a distillery at 55 Cowcross Street in London, next to present-day Farringdon Station. From their base in Clerkenwell,

Booth's grew to be the biggest distilling firm in the UK, and another distillery was built by Sir Felix Booth in Brentford, Essex, in 1817. Booth's is currently owned by spirits giant Diageo, and as of 2006 is manufactured under the supervision of 'Booth's Distilleries of London' in Plainfield, Illinois. But putting the inconvenience of geography aside, Booth's is still the oldest gin brand in production today.

The year 1769 saw perhaps the biggest name in gin establish a distillery in Bermondsey, south London. Deciding it was better to keep his competitors closer, Alexander Gordon moved his entire operation to 67-68 Goswell Road in 1786. By the end of the 18th century Gordon's was producing over half a million gallons of gin from Goswell Road. Despite mergers with Tanqueray and a sale to DCL, which went on to be known as Diageo, production remained on the same site at Goswell Road right up until the late 1980s.

One of the oldest and most significant families of the age (at least as far as the history of gin is concerned) was Boord. The Boord distillery was built in 1726, just on the cusp of the gin craze proper. But it weathered the storm and later became famous for its brand of Old Tom gin which, in 1849 started to feature the 'Cat and Barrel' trademark on the label. Boord was actually the first gin to be trademarked and its use of the cat is thought to be the springboard for the Old Tom style of gin (page 132).

Now with respectable names on the bottles and a higher standard of liquid inside them, the idea of gin was slowly becoming more palatable to the public. For business operators, there was commercial value in making gin too, which meant that it was attracting the attention of distillers outside of London too.

James Stein (father of Robert Stein, inventor of one of the first continuous stills) installed a gin plant at his Kilbagie distillery in Fife, Scotland. New distilleries in Bristol, such as the one on Cheese Lane, which was established in 1761, leveraged the nearby docks which had historically handled the lion's share of Britain's wine and sherry imports. By 1825 Bristol would have five distilleries and if they weren't making gin themselves, they would certainly be selling the spirit on to be re-distilled as such. Similar things were going on in Liverpool. The Vauxhall Distillery was founded in 1781 by Robert Preston, followed by the Bank Hall Distillery, the original site being located very near the present-day Liverpool Gin Distillery in Kirkdale.

Meanwhile, in one of Britain's most important commercial shipping ports, Plymouth, one Mr. Coates joined the Fox & Williamson Distillery in 1793. He bought the operation some time after, renaming the distillery Coates & Co and began selling his own Plymouth Gin.

ABOVE The gentlemen of gin brought advertising clout, drawing attention to their (supposed) history and accolades.

THE RISE OF THE GIN PALACE

As we move in to the 19th century, it's worth reviewing the drinking habits across the entire class spectrum at that time. The upper classes, free from the constraints of cost, continued to enjoy anything imported: wines, spirits, genever (or 'Hollands gins'), rum, brandy, and in the not-too-distant-future, cocktails. The high price of these products was often more about availability rather than quality, but being expensive they at least gave the illusion of quality and earned the imbiber some valuable ranking points amongst their peers.

The middle classes stuck mostly to ales and porter (notwithstanding the occasional imported spirit or liqueur, you understand), enjoying them in their taverns, public house and clubs.

For the poor, as Patrick Dillon's book *The Much Lamented Death of Madame Geneva* puts it, 'Freed from the tyranny of Madame Geneva the poor seemed to eagerly embrace middle class virtues.' Beer had always been the drink of the poor, but the cut-price gin touted during the craze period had been an opportunity too great to miss out on. Following the gin craze, home-grown liquor options like gin and whisky were still many people's first (or only) available option, so consumption remained steady but not outrageous. Things were set to change, however, as the beginning of the 19th century saw the price of beer rise quite sharply.

This wouldn't have been too much of a problem if it weren't for some disastrous legislation in the pipeline (are you seeing a pattern here?). The early 1800s saw the British government fight a long and dirty war with smugglers and illicit distillers, many of whom were

ABOVE The gin palace was a melting pot of inebriety, where gin was stacked high and sold cheap with little concern for class, age or gender.

born into the game of making and moving contraband items into and around the country. Whisky smuggling was dealt with in the 1823 Excise Act, which successfully curtailed the 14,000 illicit operations thought to be operating in Scotland at the time.

Gin was next on the list and the solution came two years later, in 1825, when the government slashed the cost of a distilling licence and cut duties by a whopping 40%. This was partly in an effort to legitimize (and tax) all illicit operations, and partly to ameliorate the economic impact of the grain surplus that Britain was experiencing. But with the lower classes already on the hunt for a high-strength, low-cost alternative to beer, it didn't take long before, with tails between legs, the poor flocked in the direction of their old friend Madame Geneva.

Between 1825 and 1826, gin consumption doubled from 3.7 million gallons to 7.4 million gallons. Once again, a pint of gin was cheaper than a pint of beer, and for the present time, even easier to get your hands on, too.

Distilleries caught on quickly and some bought up taverns in central London, which they fitted out with ornate panels of cut glass, gas lighting and long polished bars. Frequented by all classes save for the higher echelons, gin palaces became the grand meeting halls of apathetic gin drinkers, and the pit-stop for those after a quick fix or a 'flash of lightning' before heading home or on to the theatre.

Going on appearances alone, the gin palace was as far removed from the shady goings-on of a gloomy gin house as one could imagine, and a spectacular piece of 19th-century mass marketing at the point of sale. From the outside, the gin palace must have appeared a jewel amongst the sooty gloom of London's urban landscape. The comparatively large frontage would be clad with plate glass windows adorned with stucco roses, gas lamps hung from the walls and the signage was embellished with golden flourishes.

Appearances can be, and in this case, were, deceiving though. Looking every bit the sumptuous playground for pleasure seekers and gin connoisseurs, this gilded dram shop was more a toxic sump, an enabler, designed and built with large volumes of people, gin and profits in mind.

Gin was stored in enormous wooden vats, which were stored above the bar, ready for administration to the poor creatures that jostled around, with children and animals underfoot, like cattle to a trough. Brandishing seductive names like 'Cream of the Valley' and 'Best Butter Gin', the marketing engine was hard at work. There were no seats. This was fast-food liquor. In truth, the gin palace was nothing more than a gin shop with a facelift. The product of a political mistake more than the need for decadent surroundings to drink in.

The popularity of the gin palace was as fervent as it was short-lived. The government corrected their legislative blunder in 1830, reducing the tax on beer, provoking a mass exodus from the gin palaces as the taverns and public houses resumed normal service. But the legacy of the gin palace persisted. Taverns upped their game, taking some design cues from the gin palaces and cutting the template for the Victorian pubs that can still be seen in London and beyond.

NEW STYLES EMERGE

By the mid-19th century, gin in England had, with heavy steps, left behind the turpentine-laced gut-rot of the gin craze, and settled upon the still-rough-around-the-edges-but-just-about-drinkable gin palace tipple. The 'gentlemen of gin' deserved a pat on the back. Salt of vitriol and alum were crossed off the shopping list in place of more 'natural' options like angelica root, which cemented the status of these dependable family-owned brands and improved gin's marketability no end. The gin palaces had been a nasty bump in the road in terms of category credibility, but no one could deny that they did a sterling job of placing the product in the consumer's hands. Now, if gin was going to have any kind of future challenging the superior character and quality of genever, sherry and brandy, it was going to have to face up to some hard truths.

Firstly, gin had always been a bit of a patch-up job in that botanicals were used as an 'air freshener' to cover up the 'bad smell' of the base spirit. The production methods of the base spirit hadn't evolved in three centuries. It was still produced in batches using large pot stills and little consideration was given to how it actually tasted. Dealing with the problem at the root was needed, so the pursuit of a higher-quality base spirit that could be produced at scale became a driving force for many entrepreneurial distillers of that time.

One of the first of these was French chemist Edouard Adam, who developed and patented the first type of column still in 1804. Unrecognizable from previous stills, Adam's column was a horizontal arrangement that linked together a series of what Adam called 'large eggs', with pipes that would route alcohol vapour from one to the next. The strength of the spirit increased in each subsequent egg, whilst the leftover stuff was recycled back at the start again.

Next came the Pistorius Still, patented in 1817, which was the first still to be arranged in a column shape. Steam was pumped up from the bottom and beer from the top and distillation took place on a series of perforated 'plates' arranged through the length of the column. This design worked best because it allowed for a smooth graduation of temperature change from higher at the bottom to lower at the top. Since ethyl alcohol boils at exactly 78.3°C (172.9°F), in theory you could extract spirit vapour off the column at a height that corresponded to that temperature and capture a very high-strength spirit, leaving most of the (undesirable) residual flavour behind.

Subsequent iterations were developed by the French engineer Jean-Baptiste Cellier Blumenthal and then Robert Stein, who owned the Kilbagie Distillery in Fife, Scotland. By 1830 the final design had been reached, fully realized in a design patented by the Irish excise officer, Aeneas Coffey. The 'Coffey Still' or 'Patent Still', as it would be later known, was a truly continuous process, where beer was pumped in and high-strength alcohol drawn off. It was energy-efficient for its time, using the cool pipes that fed beer into the system as condensing coils for the hot alcohol vapours exiting it. It was a work of genius for its time, so much so that the basic design is used all over the world today. Coffey's company was registered in 1835, but later, in 1872, under the management of Aeneas' son, Aeneas, the company was handed over to the site foreman, John Dore. John Dore & Co. continue to make stills today, awarding them the title of the 'oldest manufacturer of distillery equipment in the world'.

The promise of a higher-strength, more neutral-tasting base spirit, was the secret to the next stage of the evolutionary process. Better spirits meant that fewer botanicals were needed in the cover-up job and it also meant that less sugar – which was by no means cheap at the time – was required. Gin would become drier, more delicate and – dare I say it – aromatic. And good gin couldn't have come at a better time either. Genever from both Holland and Belgium was under a trade embargo during the Napoleonic Wars (1803–1815), so Britain was forced to turn to native options.

It was around this time that England's first truly credible gin style emerged: Old Tom. Steeped in legend (quite literally as some might have you believe) this style could be described as a slightly more botanical heavy, and perhaps slightly sweeter, 'cordial', version of the London Dry Gins that we drink today. Theories on the Old Tom name are bounteous and colourful, including a tall tale of a tom cat falling into a vat of gin, imparting its 'flavour' in its death throws and lending Old Tom another slang name, 'cat's water'. The more plausible claim for the name comes from Hodge's Distillery in the London Borough of Lambeth. The proprietor was one 'Old' Thomas Chamberlain, who helped fund the opening of a gin palace in Covent Garden. The owner was Thomas Norris, a former employee at Hodge's. Norris bought a particular recipe from Chamberlain, which was reserved only for his top customers. Norris's gin palace kept it in big barrels above the bar marked with 'Old Tom's Gin'. Old Tom would go on to become a catch-all term for the style of gin that was drunk during that time.

Adulterations Detected, an 1857 manual on how to detect fraudulent spirits, compares recipes for London and Plymouth gins, where the recipe for 'Plain or London Gin' includes '700 gallons of the second rectification, 70 lbs German juniper berries, 70 lbs coriander seeds, 3.5 lbs almond cake, 1.5 lbs angelica root, 6 lbs liquorice powder' whereas 'West Country Gin, known as Plymouth Gin' is made from the same quantity of spirit and only '14 lbs German juniper berries, 1.5 lbs calamus root and 8 lbs sulphuric acid'. The London Gin recipe appears, at first, to be closer in style to the gins we drink today and would certainly have produced a more concentrated product. But it's possible that, even though both recipes contain no sugar at all, the London Gin would seem more like an Old Tom than a London Dry thanks to its high concentration of botanical ingredients. Plymouth omits the sweet botanicals, but also uses less juniper too, which gives weight to the brand's claim of being the world's first 'dry gin'.

New distillation methods did not go unnoticed in Holland and Belgium. In 1830, a revolt by the southern Low Countries established the borders for modern-day Belgium and The Netherlands. The first move of the sovereign Belgian government was to ban the importation of genever from Holland and lower taxes on their own home-brew. Belgium was finally entering a well-earned genever renaissance after 250 years of war, embargo, prohibition and underrepresentation.

The Belgians were quick to adopt new practices, such as Cellier Blumenthal's column still, and production capability quickly reached eye-watering levels. The late, great Meeus Distillery, established in

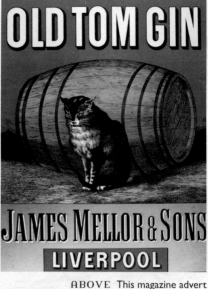

ABOVE This magazine advert from the 1920s makes it clear which version of the Old Tom story it's going for.

Antwerp in 1869, could output 50,000 litres (13,200 US gallons) of spirit a day. 1912 saw an all-time record of 100,000,000 litres (26.4 million US gallons) of Belgian spirit flow off the stills. To put that into context, it's roughly the same volume of liquid as Gordon's, Tanqueray, Beefeater and Bombay Sapphire sold together in 2014.

The Dutch on the other hand were slower to adopt the distillation column, which meant their product still relied heavily on malt wine and sat very much in the Oude style, for now at least. Fortunately, the Dutch were pretty good at making malt wine – so good, in fact, that English, German and French distillers imported it for use as the base for their own spirits and liqueurs. The 20th century would be a very unkind period for genever, however, with the Great Depression and World Wars around the corner.

GIN IS JUST THE TONIC

To discover the distant origins of the G&T, we must first investigate the roots of tonic water, or the 'bark' of tonic water, to be more specific. Tonic is little more than sweetened and acidulated fizzy water, but it contains one key ingredient: quinine. Quinine is an effective painkiller, a good antipyretic (fever-reducer) and a particularly proficient antimalarial.

Quinine is naturally produced by the *Cinchona* tree. There are 90 or so varieties of this red-barked tree, which also happens to be a relative of the coffee tree. Peruvian cinchona bark was first brought to Europe in or around 1631, during a time when even the best medical minds were completely clueless when it came to both the cause and treatment for 'marsh fever' or 'the ague' as malaria was then called.

The miraculous story of cinchona's discovery goes something like this: some time in the early 17th century, the Countess of Chinchón, the wife of the Viceroy of Peru, became very sick with tertian fever (a form of malaria that recurs every second day). The Countess was a popular celebrity of her day so this spelled bad times for Peru, and stories of the Countess' sickness spread from Lima through to other colonies, including the Andean hill town of Loxa. The Prefect of Loxa travelled to Lima, met with the Viceroy and prescribed a special remedy to the Countess, derived from the

LEFT Cinchona revolutionized the art of medicine and gave us tonic water for our gin!

bark of an indigenous tree. The countess recovered and the tree from which the bark originated was renamed 'cinchona' in her honour.

There's only one tiny problem with that story, though: it's a complete fabrication. Indeed, the Countess was never even ill in the first place, that is, until she died suddenly in 1641 on a trip to Madrid. Detailed diaries left by the Viceroy's secretary make very little reference to malaria at all, and offer no clues of magical remedies made from tree bark.

Another possible scenario sees the Incas passing on their knowledge of the tree (under duress, or otherwise) to the Spanish conquistadors. The best and oldest reference we have to cinchona's medicinal properties comes from an Augustinian Friar by the name of Antonio de la Calancha, who wrote in 1638: 'A tree grows which they call the fever tree in the country of Loxa whose bark, of the colour of cinnamon colour, made into powder to the weight of two small silver coins and given as a beverage cures the fever and tertianas; it has produced miraculous results in Lima.'

Another priest, Bernabé Cobó, wrote a similar account the following year, describing the tonic as 'a bit coarse and very bitter' and advising that 'those powders must be taken [...] in wine or any other liquor'.

What we know for sure is that by the turn of the 18th century, cinchona bark powder was being used widely as an antimalarial drug, often being added to wine and sherry to mask its intensely bitter flavour. Bernardo Rammazzini was the chief physician to the Duke of Modena, and in 1707 he wrote that 'Cinchona revolutionized the art of medicine as profoundly as gunpowder had the art of war.'

The Spanish controlled all of the world's supply of quinine up until the 19th century, and it wasn't until the Dutch managed to plant trees in Java, and the British in India, that the medicine became widely available among the colonies. Quinine was first isolated in France, in 1820, and quinine pills were made available by the Philadelphia-based firm Rosengarten & Sons, in 1823. For most people, this advancement meant a huge sigh of relief, as it eliminated any need to drink the bitter tonic any longer. But by that time British troops in the Indian colonies had already developed a work-around. By mixing their tonic with sugar and gin, the whole thing became not just tolerable, but enjoyable. West Indian workers digging out the Panama canal half a century later did a similar thing, mixing their quinine pills with pink lemonade and gin. This would have seemed every bit the double-bonus in the eyes of the recipients. Gin was still regarded as a health drink in the 19th century. Not a cure-all, but perhaps equivalent to a daily dose of multivitamins. In 1890, The London Medical Recorder made no bones about where they stood on the matter, 'Our attention has been recently called to the "Original Plymouth Gin". As this Medical Recorder will circulate amongst the profession in India, we have no hesitation in calling attention to its value for medicinal, as well as general use.'

Erasmus Bond marketed the first commercially-available tonic water brand in 1858. He was quickly followed by Jean Jacob Schweppe, who had previously launched the world's first carbonated water in 1770. Schweppes original seltzer waters were available in no less than five varying degrees of fizziness, each purported to offer different medicinal benefits. Schweppe's have been masters of fizz for nearly 250 years now.

When I first explored making my own tonic water, back in 2005 (pages 146–149), the only mixers available in the UK came from Schweppes and Britvic. There are now over a dozen options that are readily available to buy online or in supermarkets. The growth in this category began with the launch of Fever Tree, who quite rightly recognised that 'when three-quarters of your gin and tonic is tonic, make sure you use the best'. Whether the best tonic is Fever Tree or another brand is a subjective matter – the refreshing reality of the

ABOVE British soldiers receiving their daily dose of quinine during World War I.

RIGHT This 1920s advert was designed by William Barribal, a leading Art Deco illustrator of the day.

situation may be that there isn't a one-size-fits-all tonic brand and that, just as each gin has a unique botanical profile, so too does it have an ideal tonic partner. An antidote to match the poison, if you like – but it would be Fever Tree and East Imperial (which has quite possibly the best standalone flavour) that get crosses on my ballot paper. With 'craft tonic' in high demand, and bartenders coming under increasing pressure to diversify their tonic water stocks, the natural evolution was flavoured tonic water. You can now take your pick from familiar sounding and naturally fitting flavours as elderflower, lemon and liquorice/licorice or the more esoteric options like 'Mediterranean' and 'herbal'. Amazingly, cinchona trees remain the only economically practical source of quinine, and even cut-price brands of tonic water are still made from quinine extracted from cinchona bark.

But perhaps one of the most unrecognized factors in choosing good tonic is how damn fizzy the thing is. Ice and gin will suck the fizz right out of your tonic, and in my option no other brand can match Schweppes for sheer face-melting carbonic impact – impossible volumes of CO_2 tenant every bottle.

A PUNCH AND A KICK

By the time Harry Craddock's *The Savoy Cocktail Book* was published in 1930, gin had become the most dependable weapon in the cocktail bartender's arsenal. Craddock's 'masters thesis' lists 750 cocktail recipes and over half of them contain gin of one sort or another: gin; dry gin; Plymouth gin; and Old Tom gin. Martinis were in full flow, Slings in full swing, and Fizzes showing no signs of fizzling out. Gin was experiencing its golden age.

But it hadn't been all plain sailing to get there. Gin's graduation to cocktail stardom featured all the distasteful experiences and dirty encounters of any awkward adolescent period. Hampered by the inconvenience of being a second rate product, and used to ill-effect in various examples of early bartending explorations, gin was by no means the original cocktail spirit – that honour went to brandy and whisky – but it was perhaps the bartender's most capable test subject.

The punch pre-dates the cocktail by at least 200 years, but 'Gin Punch' would have a somewhat oxymoronic term in the 18th century. Punch, which contained such lavish ingredients as lemons and oranges shipped in from Asia, spices and sugar from

LEFT The frightfully agreeable and convivial goings-on of a punch bowl caucus room.

the Caribbean colonies, as well as imported brandy or rum, was, at up to 8 shillings a bowl, very expensive indeed. English gin, on the other hand, was the widely abused crack of the scrabbling masses, and as we have already learned, incredibly cheap to boot. Needless to say, throwing gin into a punch was an act of madness, like dropping a spoon of heroin into a glass of Burgundy. But they did it, and in doing so opened up the world of punch to a whole new middle-class audience who were happy to fit the 1 shilling bar tab for a tainted taste of high society.

There are no known recipes for Gin Punch from the 18th century (a fact for which we should probably be grateful) but since gin punch may have been mixed from either imported Holland's gin or inferior English gin the intended purpose of the concoction seems to have varied widely. One English journal from 1749 suggests that Gin Punch (made, presumably, on this occasion from English gin) might not have even been fit for human consumption, recommending that a 'hornful of gin punch' be used in a recipe that cures 'distemper among cattle'. References to its use in non-bestial medicine become more frequent towards the end of the 18th century, where gin punch is used to treat kidney stones, promote perspiration, fix weakness, cure beriberi (nutritional deficit) and many other things besides.

Higher quality punches were of course available and it's more likely that the punch consumed in 1776, by James Boswell, the Scottish lawyer and biographer of Samuel Johnson, was made from imported stuff. Boswell wrote in his diary a favourable account of a nighttime encounter with gin, and more specifically with, the gin punch, 'I drank rather too much gin punch. It was a new liquor to me, and I liked it much.'

As the Georgian period drew to a close and the gin palaces opened for trading, we begin to see recipes for gin punch. The earliest of these come from neither the gin palaces nor the physician's handbook, but from London's tobacco-stained gentlemen's clubs like Limmer's Hotel and the Garrick Club and, curiously, from Oxford University.

ABOVE The Garrick Club was 'where actors and men of refinement and education might meet on equal terms'. They also drank punch.

Oxford Nightcaps (1827) was a 30-page pamphlet commissioned by Oxford University, which lists various weird and wonderful recipes. It has a strong case for 'the world's first cocktail book' – or book dedicated only to mixed drinks – and in it we encounter a recipe for 'Gin Punch' made using 2 pints of gin, oranges, lemons, capillaire (a kind of sugar syrup aromatized with orange flower water) and white wine. That's it. Nothing out of the ordinary there... oh, wait... it also called for calves-feet jelly, which was a kind of primitive gelatine substitute made from boiling up the feet of baby cows. Delicious.

A more approachable drink came in the form of the Garrick Club Punch, which emanated from the Leicester Square club of the same name that opened in 1831. The club's manager, an American by the name of Stephen Price, was an early advocate of iced soda water, which would have seemed a strange combination at the time, as David Wondrich notes in *Punch* (2011) 'soda water [was] a popular hangover cure... seen as an antidote to punch, not an accomplice.' The Garrick Club Punch recipe – which includes 'half a pint of gin, lemon peel, lemon juice, sugar, maraschino, a pint and a quarter of water, and two bottles of iced soda water' – was published in *London Quarterly* in 1835 and over the years that followed it became an international sensation, laying the foundations for the Limmer's Punch and eventually the John Collins and Tom Collins single-serve equivalents that took America by storm in the 1870s.

There are eight recipes for Gin Punch in William Terrington's *Cooling Cup and Dainty Drinks* (1869) including the Punch 'à la Garrick' and Terrington's own 'Gin Punch à la Terrington', which replaces Maraschino in the Garrick Club Punch with Green Chartreuse. Here is a book that was clearly intended only for those with some serious capital to dispose of on their drinking pleasures, listing such luxury commodities as pineapple syrup and green tea, and even going as far as to distinguish between German seltzer water, 'aerated lemonade' and Vichy water, then providing instructions on how to make and source various types of ice. Terrington's inclusion of gin in the book is a striking indicator of how much the English gin category had accomplished in the decades that precede the book. And his specification of 'good unsweetened gin' leaves us with little doubt that this was probably not genever, but English gin. The shift from sweet through to dry, in England at least, was finally gathering pace.

The punch bowl served as the perfect societal seasoning to witty, high-spirited gatherings among friends, and genial discussion on politics with business associates. Punches scribed out a playing field on which the sport of mixing drinks could be enjoyed, but the invention of the cocktail put an end to it being a team game. Despite featuring a good array of punch drinks, both Terrington's book and *Jerry Thomas' Bartender's Guide* focused more on the single serve punch than their predecessors did, before deviating entirely to cocktails, which would be the modus operandi for cocktail authors over the next 50 years. There's a certain sadistic pleasure that can be taken in witnessing the manifestation of one's own, personal drink through the deft movements of a trained bartender. And so it was that the future of mixed drinks lay not in the murky waters of the English punch bowl, but in the icy embrace of an American cocktail glass.

THE AMERICAN DRINK

America stuck to genever for most of the 19th century. This was thanks, in part, to the large numbers of Dutch immigrants (Manhattan was New Amsterdam before it was New York), bringing their higher-quality spirit and superior distilling skillset with them. During the 19th century, five times as much 'Holland's Gin' was imported into the US compared to English gin. The gin distilleries that were established in the US during this time followed suit, and mostly copied the 'Holland's Gin' approach, even labelling their product as such, which on more than one occasion landed them in legal bother. America needed gin, as a growing trend towards cocktails, thanks in part to the availability of ice from the 1830s and the invention of the cocktail shaker in the 1840s, meant that America was thirsty. That most patriotic of American spirits, whiskey, was top of the mixing list, followed closely by imported brandy, but gin distilleries sprung up too to meet demand and establish a market, and by 1851 there were six distillers in Brooklyn, producing a combined 2.9 million gallons of grain spirit, most of it destined for rectification into gin.

The American distilling manual, *Hall's Distiller* (1813), which boasts

LEFT American brands like Fleischmann's were liquid proof of the nation's shift towards drier, steely spirits.

an entire chapter on 'Full and particular directions for imitating Holland's gin', provides us with an insight into the state of gin and genever in America during the early 19th century: 'The use of spirits of turpentine has unfortunately become too common, and is one great cause of the badness of American gin', then asking 'why can we not make gin equal to Holland? The superiority of their gin is generally attributed to some secret, known only to themselves.' In the book, Hall offered detailed practical advice to distillers on how best to adjust their practices towards the Dutch style.

In 1870, the first dry gin distillery opened in North America. It was founded by Charles and Maximilian Fleischmann, a Czech family of distillers and brewers who emigrated to the US in the 1860s. Based in Cincinnati, Ohio, the brothers had already became quite famous for their compressed yeast, and became the biggest yeast manufacturer in the world. Charles' son, Julius, became Mayor of Cincinnati at 28, and their gin, along with every other branch of their rapidly growing empire, enjoyed great success. The gin is still available today, and owned by the Sazerac Co.

The switch to dry gin in America was ploddingly gradual. The earliest cocktail books, like *Jerry Thomas's The Bartender's Guide* (1862), specified 'Holland's gin' and 'Old Tom', but where no specification is made one can be assured that genever was the implied ingredient. And I'm talking proper genever, 100% malt wine, with no short-measure oak influence in the mix. For the contemporary, conscientious bartender, whose profession relies on an understanding of the flavour profile of classic cocktails like the Gin Fizz and Tom Collins, this revelation throws everything into disarray, fundamentally altering these bastions of the cocktail world. As spirits writer David Wondrich notes, 'This makes perfect sense: in the days before the dominance of the Dry Martini, when gin was drunk in slings, simple punches or cocktails (the original kind, with bitters and sugar), the mellow, malty roundness of the "Hollands", as it was known, was preferable to the steely sharpness of a London Dry Gin, or even an Old Tom, which stood somewhere between the two styles.'

Harry Johnson's Bartender's Manual (1888) has 19 gin drinks, 11 that call for Hollands, eight with Old Tom. One of those eight is for a 'Martine Cocktail', which is considered by many to be a typo on the 'e', and therefore the first recipe for a Martini (page 142). William Schmidt's *The Flowing Bowl* (1892) has 11 genever drinks in it and only five with Old Tom, and by 1908, the transformation to dry was in full flow, with the publication of Bill 'Cocktail' Boothby's *The World's Drinks and How to Mix Them*, which featured nine genever drinks, nine Old Tom drinks and six drinks that called for 'dry gin'.

The Volstead Act of 1919 brought about national prohibition in America between 1920–1933 and forced the closure of thousands of saloons, cocktail bars, breweries and distilleries. It could have marked the end of the cocktail, and it certainly set the American cocktail back by a decade or so, but it also forced it to become a global entity, as talented bartenders exported their trade to Europe and beyond.

BELOW This 1929 drawing depicts Prohibition officers interrupting the exploits of boozy passengers aboard the 'Majestic' upon its arrival in New York.

The upshot of this sudden and imperative propagation of knowledge and skill elevated bars like those at The Savoy and The Café Royal in London and The Ritz in Paris to historic standards. The bartenders who ran these operations became the next generation of superstar drinks mixers, and the names of Harry McElhone and Harry Craddock secured their positions in drinking history.

ABOVE The legendary Harry Craddock mixes a cocktail in the 1930s. Interestingly, one of the ingredients he is using appears to be genever.

The early 20th century saw the conception of some of the classic gin cocktails, like the Bronx (1905), the Dry Martini (1906) and the Aviation (1916). Then, in Europe and abroad, the Negroni (c. 1920), the Singapore Sling (c. 1922), the Hanky Panky (c. 1925) and the Pegu Club (c. 1927).

From British gin's perspective, prohibition was not all bad news. Determined distillers explored new means and ways of bootlegging their product on to US soil, fuelled by a desire to secure the gin industry (which by this time had become heavily reliant on the lucrative American market) while at the same time scoring valuable kudos points that would be cashed in during the 1930s when Gordon's and Gilbey's both established distilleries on American soil. Prohibition saw enterprising smugglers transport gin by way of the Bahamas and Canada, but the risks involved meant that product fetched a high price. Meanwhile, those who couldn't gain access to the contraband product, or couldn't afford it, set about making their own. Gin was the obvious DIY candidate, as history had already proven, so turpentine once again assumed the role of the juniper berry, and bathtubs the role of the still.

GIN'S DARK AGE

The return to cocktails after prohibition was an uneasy experience for Americans. Prohibition had brought out the worst in drinkers, and forced them to explore the depths of drinking depravity that they never would have thought possible. How could things go back to the way they were when all the artistry of the cocktail had been so easily forgotten?

America sought shelter in that most trusted and iconic of all cocktails, the Martini. The 'Cocktail Hour' was conceived, or rather concocted, in an effort to encourage Americans back into bars and ordering cocktails. Even though the Martini was experiencing its glory days, and would continue for some time to do so, even after World War II, the creativity and showmanship of the bartender was nowhere to be found. Not a single decent gin cocktail was invented between 1935 and 1980. But for the time being, gin had bigger problems to contend with.

World War II saw restrictions on the sale of spirits imposed across all sides of the Atlantic Ocean. In Great Britain, gin distilleries were requisitioned to produce industrial acetone, which was required for the manufacture of cordite, an essential propellant used in shell and rifle cartridges. Rather fittingly, the best product to extract acetone from is that most lethal of playground weaponry, the horse chestnut, or 'conker'. In the US, many distilleries were seized and repurposed to produce industrial alcohol to use as fuel for submarines' torpedoes, although some would argue that the American whiskey industry benefited greatly from a few extra years of maturation in their casks.

Despite Belgium and The Netherlands' early attempts to remain neutral during World War II, much of the copper in their stills was seized by the invading Nazi forces and used for the manufacture of munitions. Some distilleries employed ingenious tactics to protect their equipment – Filliers, for example, hid their copper in nearby lakes to keep it safe from the German war effort.

In Belgium, a radical ban on selling genever in Belgian bars as a means of combating excessive alcohol consumption was enforced in 1919. It would go on to last for a remarkable 66 years. This coincided with the US embarking upon their 'noble experiment' that saw Prohibition law imposed for a full 13 years. The Belgian genever ban more closely mirrored the absinthe ban of 1915 in France, however, where the

ABOVE The end of Prohibition saw drinkers return to bars, but the damage was done – the cocktail's golden era was coming to an end.

government took the misguided approach of victimising and driving out the most popular drink, blind to the fact that alcoholics will drink anything they can get their hands on. With no genever available the Belgians turned to beer instead. But genever's loss was beer's gain, and it was during this period that the Belgian beer industry rose up to become the best in the world, as it still remains today. It seems incredible that entire generations of drinking-age Belgians lived out their lives with very limited access to their country's national spirit.

The memory of Belgian genever began to fade from the minds of drinkers, both at home and beyond the country's borders, while the Dutch spirit surged on in popularity. It's for this reason that we tend

ABOVE Vodka was the white warrior, the Soviet slayer, the faceless phantom. It exploded during the 1950s.

to associate genever with The Netherlands, rather than Belgium. Having said that, in time the Dutch too would stumble. Aggressive genever price wars during the late 1960s caused the industry to cannibalize itself, forcing distillers to cut corners and ultimately allowing the jonge style to rise as the victor.

In the UK, Brits turned back to the G&T, but it quickly fell out of fashion through the 1960s, replaced by cheap and sweet continental wines, blended scotch and sherry. The G&T became the preserve of the aristocracy, the perception being that they were only consumed at garden parties, on board yachts, or on the occasion that 'one' visits the queen for afternoon tea. Meanwhile, in America, drinkers once again returned their attentions to the Martini, which had become consistently drier over the past couple of decades.

The post-war drinking milieu was reflected in the progressive changes in culture that the war had brought about. Sweet and flabby Old Tom was fast becoming old-hat, and its exit made way for the stiff and steely London Dry style – named after the city which first campaigned the style – and it became the new hero of the highball. But the legend was short-lived, as a new player was about to enter the game.

Just like Ian Fleming's legendary secret-service agent who helped to make it famous, vodka was packed full of delicious anonymity and seasoned with no short measure of thrilling danger. Coinciding neatly with the Cold War period, Russian vodka offered something exotic and non-conformist to the latest generation of drinkers. Brands such as Smirnoff first landed on American shores in the 1940s, sporting the marketing tag line 'It leaves you breathless', a clever ploy aimed as much at those wishing to conceal a sneaky drink under odourless breath, as it was to those people looking for a stimulating social lubricant. The campaign had the desired effect, and vodka sales in the US increased 100-fold between 1950 and 1956, from 40,000 cases to an eye-watering 4 million cases. Vodka was leaping past gin and, in time, would go on to surpass even whiskey too.

And so the battle was lost. Gin was perceived to be old-fashioned and its marketing had been comprehensively outclassed. Even though sales remained steady in America throughout the 1970s and 1980s, there was no question that this period of the 20th century belonged to vodka. All that was left was for gin to hunker down, assess the damage, watch and wait. Its time would come again.

THE RETURN OF GIN

These days gin remains a quintessentially British drink, although it is probably with the English that the strongest association lies. According to the International Wine & Spirit Record (IWSR) though, Brits are not the biggest consumers of gin – we quaffed a paltry 400 ml/13½ fl. oz. of gin per person in 2014. If, like me, you're known to put away similar quantities on a single afternoon, you may be surprised by that figure, but still, it places us (I am a Brit) at fifth in the world per capita.

In fourth place is Spain, which has, for some time, been an important market for premium gin brands like Beefeater and

BELOW A selection of some of the finest gins around today, in all their shapes, colours and sizes.

Tanqueray. In third place is The Netherlands where roughly one standard 70-cl (24-fl. oz.) bottle is consumed per person, per year. Then it's Slovakia in second with 1.2 litres (41 fl. oz.) per person. First place goes to the mighty Philippines, who drink more gin by volume than any other nation, drowning in a very respectable 1.4 litres (47 fl. oz.) of gin per person every year – around six times that of the USA. (If all this is beginning to sound a bit boozy, keep in mind that the Russians put away a whopping 14 litres (3⅔ US gallons) of vodka per person every year.)

Gin has reached the most exciting period along what has been, by any standards, a highly tumultuous journey from its origins as a medieval cure-all tonic, to the tables of the wealthy and powerful, on to battlefields and into new kingdoms. It has gorged on the poor and cruelly seduced the vulnerable, then risen up to become the most trusted of cocktail ingredients, before succumbing to the worst of all fates: obscurity.

There are many threads that support the gin revival story. There can be no doubt that a certain blue glass bottle marked the beginning, though; Bombay Sapphire did a number on all of us with a double jab of luxury and authenticity, followed by an upper-cut of fresh, accessible flavour. As the 1990s drew to a close, the cavalry began to gather. Backed up by the stalwarts of Beefeater, Tanqueray, Seagram's and Gordon's, Citadelle from France and Hendrick's from Scotland became the next heroes of the tale, quickly followed up by Junipero, Martin Miller's, Hayman's and Sipsmith.

For new distilleries and products to flourish so effectively and repeatedly, there must first be a market. That market came about largely through the rediscovery of classic cocktail culture, along with 1930s and 1950s couture, which in turn has led to the new wave of bars where the emphasis is on quality of drinks and service, as well as provenance and authenticity of the ingredients used. Bartenders are more aware of their ingredients than they have ever been, and certainly in terms of technique and professionalism, they are better trained, too. This awareness of product, as well as inquisition in to the history of mixology, has formed a gap in the market for dynamic, young products that aim to either innovate the category, or re-create the past.

The craft distilling movement has altered the landscape of the spirits world, which was only until quite recently dominated by large, cumbersome, corporations. Craft distilling (as with brewing, and indeed, any other craft activity) works on so many levels, supporting the small guy, supporting local industry, exercising freedom for the producer to innovate and broadening the scope of the category. In the US and UK alone, an average of two distilleries a week opened in 2015.

But the craft movement is by no means limited to these markets. Spirits enthusiasts, brewers, engineers and crackpot scientists are establishing gin distilleries across virtually every developed nation on the planet. I recently heard that there are now seven gin distilleries in Portugal, a country that had none only 10 years ago. Many of these new operations are unashamedly using gin as a go-between to help with cashflow while they age whisky, rum or brandy stock. But many others see gin playing a pivotal role in their future businesses.

Gins are now being made in over 30 countries, and in numerous different styles, incorporating hundreds of unique botanicals. London Dry, as vague as the term is, remains the supreme champion of gin styles, but past favourites like Old Tom and barrel-aged gins have been dusted off and tarted up, often revisited with unerring loyalty to their original recipes. Super and ultra premium gins now sit proudly on our liquor store shelves, encased in cut-glass packaging and adorned with various bells and whistles (the former being a true story). With price tags high enough to make your eyes water, these same bottles would have prompted laughter only a few years ago.

In the 'New Western' style gins, we're seeing an exaggeration of the category through explorations away from juniper and into floral, citrus, spice and fruit. Some new brands have adopted cutting-edge distillation processes and state-of-the-art extraction methods in pursuit of the most faithful possible liquid representation of the product. Botanicals are now foraged, juniper origin and terroir is scrutinized and production processes are laid bare for the benefit of consumer transparency.

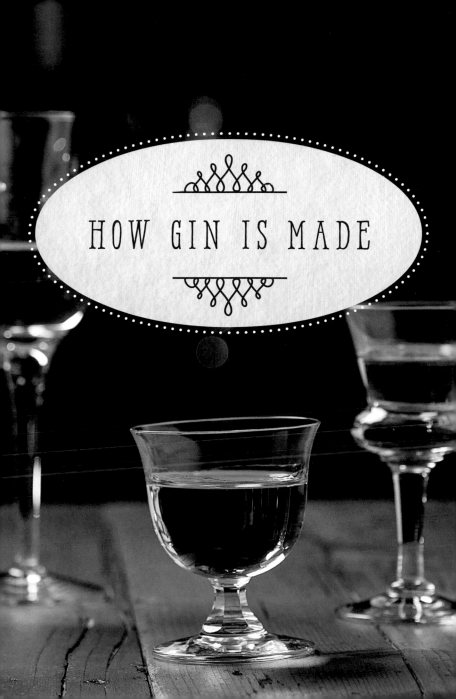

HOW GIN IS MADE

THE BASICS

Most spirits are distilled from a fermented agricultural product. Whether it's cereal, fruit or grass, the natural starch or sugars in the plant provide yeast with the fuel needed to make fermentation possible. Even through distillation, where newly formed alcohol molecules are expanded apart then wound back together again, the biological ancestry of the base product usually carries through to the liquid.

Tequila, for example, is a product of the agave plant, which lends the drink its peppery, vegetal disposition. Brandy is made from grapes, which bestow a wide range of fruit flavours upon the liquid. Malt whisky often retains some link to its humble origins as a barley grain. Bourbon's round and sweet aromas can, in part, be attributed to corn, and even that most neutral of spirits, vodka, pays some small homage to the cereal, sugar, or starch, from which it was created. Gin is the exception to this rule. The material gin is distilled from is of virtually no consequence. What is of consequence is what it is distilled with.

Gin belongs to a large family of mostly colloquially flavoured spirits and liqueurs. These spirits, which, besides gin, include a range of regional anise-flavoured spirits, as well as the caraway- and dill-flavoured akvavit of Scandinavia, are not shaped by the raw material that they were made from, but by supplemental flavours, introduced in the latter stages of production. All of these spirits are, in effect, flavoured vodkas, distilled from the fermented sugars of cereal, fruit or other plant matter. Any trace of origin is for the most part overshadowed by the botanical characteristics of fruit, vegetable, spice, grass or herb. Producing spirits in this manner bestows upon the spirits maker superior levels of control over what flavours are allowed in or out of the product and is generally a more cost-effective means of carrying flavour into the final product. Flavoured spirits like these can be manufactured using any one or combination of three distinct methods. The first is by a simple maceration.

Liqueurs are traditionally made in this way, where the subject matter (seed, bark, etc.) is steeped in spirit – usually neutral – to extract its flavour. This method extracts both flavour and colour of course, the latter of which may or may not be desirable. In the case of gin, it's a clear spirit that producers are after, so the maceration is distilled.

The second method is, technically speaking, a re-distillation, since the product has already been distilled at least once to produce a neutral spirit. During re-distillation, the vapours that boil off the maceration carry only a selected frequency of flavour through from the macerate and no colour whatsoever. The result is a concentrated perfume of volatile aromatic compounds and alcohol in a crystal-clear liquid.

The third method is to use 'off-the-shelf' compounded flavours to flavour a neutral spirit. Rather like mixing a cocktail, this process takes a lot of the hard work out of making a flavoured spirit by letting someone else do all the ground work for you. There's nothing wrong with this, of course.

Flavouring a spirit with any of the above methods results in a sharper expression of the subject than it would by fermenting and distilling it from scratch. Also, many of the botanicals used in gin production contain little or no sugar/starch, rendering them impractical or impossible to distil in the first place. For those that do, there is also a cost and practicality element to consider.

Most of the gins in this book use a combination of the first and second method. Gabriel Boudier's Saffron Gin, for example, is a distilled gin that undergoes a maceration of saffron before bottling, awarding it its golden hue. Some gins use a combination of the second and third methods. Hendrick's, for example, has a dash of compounded cucumber extract added to it after its distillation. There are no gins in this book that rely solely on the third method; this tends to be reserved for cheap supermarket brands. You could argue that they are frauds; scheming imposters who, behind all the herbal-scented bravado, are nothing more than a bunch of flavoured vodkas.

NEUTRAL SPIRIT

. . . .

All gins begin with neutral spirit. It's the blank canvass upon which the botanicals sit, the empty plate that the dish is served on, the silent space that the music fills. Neutral spirit can be made from any starch or sugar-rich agricultural product such as cereals, potatoes, grapes or molasses. Neutral spirit made from fermented cereals – corn and wheat are most common – is called sometimes called GNS (grain neutral spirit). If the starting point is cereal or potato, it is first cooked to break down the starch into sugar, but in all instances yeast is added and it is fermented into a strong beer or wine known as wash.

The distillation of neutral spirit is done in a column still. As the name suggests these workhorses of the distilling industry are big; sometimes towering many floors high. They work with a continuous feed of low-alcohol wash, which is heated by steam and forced through a series of perforated plates. Each plate acts like a still in its own right, fractioning the vapour at different levels based on its boiling point. The end result is a steady flow of nearly pure ethanol, along with plenty of waste product which is recycled back into the start of the system, to be unceremoniously stripped of its last remaining remnants of alcohol.

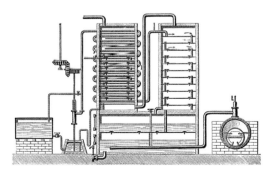

RIGHT 19th-century diagram of a column still, also called a Coffey still, after its creator, Irishman Aeneas Coffey.

In a modern pot still, it's only possible to make a spirit of around 85% alcohol by volume (ABV) and that requires multiple time-consuming distillations. 85% might sound pretty strong, and it is, but remember that if 85% of your spirit is alcohol, it means that 15% is other stuff, namely water and various residual impurities left over from fermentation. In whiskies and brandies these 'impurities' give the product character, but in gin it's the botanicals that are the stars of the show, so a clean and uncontaminated spirit is what's required.

A column still should produce a spirit of over 95% ABV (190 US proof). At that strength, so little of the character of the base material remains that the product can be deemed 'neutral'. Dilute neutral spirit with some water and you have vodka. While many vodka manufacturers will tell you that their product is not neutral in character – and as it happens, some are not – vodka is legally required to be made in this manner.

If purer is better for the purposes of making gin, why don't distillers make 100% pure alcohol? This is because at 96.48% the ethanol and water form an azeotrope – a phenomenon that occurs when the vapour of two mixed liquids has the same composition as the liquid mixture. No amount of repeated distilling will change that, although there are other means and ways of achieving 100% ethanol.

Most distilleries buy their neutral spirit in, either in large containers or drums, delivered by the tanker load. There are only a handful of gin distilleries that make their own neutral spirit, though, including Cameron Bridge (Tanqueray/Gordon's), Chase, Adnam's, Langley, Girvan (Hendrick's), G'Vine and Nolet's.

It's a matter of contention amongst distillers as to whether the base that the neutral spirit is made from has any bearing on the overall quality of the finished liquid. In the case of vodka I would say that a potato, grape, rye or barley base does produce a more nuanced liquid, but if that liquid is being distilled with a range of flavourful botanicals, I'm not convinced it makes much difference.

STEEP AND BOIL

Macerating ingredients in spirit and boiling it into aromatic vapour is the oldest and most basic form of concentrated flavour extraction via distillation. All London Dry Gins are made in this manner, and all distilled gins will undergo some degree of pot distillation where botanicals are steeped in spirit then boiled off. The heat of the boiling spirit cooks the botanicals, breaking down cell structure that holds the plant together, splitting chemical bonds and releasing aroma. The same thing happens when you cook a curry on a stove and the result in both cases is similar: the release of volatile aromatic molecules in to the surrounding atmosphere. In gin distillation the lightest of these fragrant compounds are carried upwards by the rising vapour currents. As they reach the top of the still they are drawn downwards into the lynearm (also known as the swan neck) and into the condenser. Cold water is pumped through the condenser and as the spirit vapour cools, it returns to its liquid phase forming a miscible compound of alcohol, water and aromatic components. The process may take anywhere from a couple of hours to the better part of a day. The rate of the distillation depends on a number of factors including the shape and size of the still and how aggressively the master distiller chooses to run it – all factors that will impact flavour.

The first crystal-clear drops of liquid that fall from the condenser are known as the heads, or foreshots. Because gin is made from pure neutral spirit (see left), unlike whisky or brandy, where the first 15% of the distillate may be set aside, in gin production the heads pose no significant danger. Heads can, however, contain water-insoluble compounds, derived from residual film on the inside of the still and leftovers from the previous distillation run. Traditionally distillers 'cut' the heads away based on a series of 'demisting' tests, where water is added to the spirit to see if it turns cloudy. Once the mixture remains clear the spirit can be deemed 'potable' (drinkable) and the distiller starts collecting the hearts, or the middle section

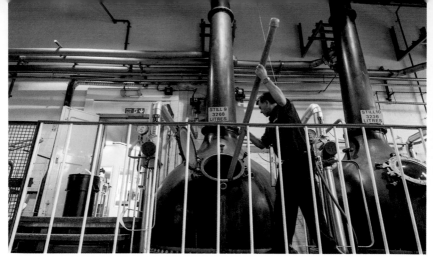

ABOVE Gin making involves macerating botanicals in neutral spirit and boiling off the aromatic vapour.

of the run. This is the first of two 'cuts' that take place during distillation, marking the beginning and the end of the spirit's recovery. Besides the gin recipe itself, the cutting of the spirit is probably the most important determinant of gin character. Some distillers claim to make these cuts with their noses, and some by feeling the liquid with their hands. In the more automated distilleries, the first cut is made routinely, at a specified time.

Once the heart of the product is distilling, the distiller can 'nose' the product. Some botanicals emerge more quickly than others. Juniper, for example, typically presents itself near the start of the spirit run, whereas coriander emerges nearer the end. As time goes on, the strength of the distillate will diminish and the aroma will lose its brightness and finesse. If left long enough, the distillate would turn to cooked botanical water vapour. Naturally it's in the best interests of the distiller to collect as much alcohol as possible, but also for it to be tasty. The timing of the second cut marks the end of spirits collection and the flow of liquid will be diverted into the feints receiver. The feints won't make it as far as the bottle, but most distilleries still collect them and re-distil them in subsequent batches, or send them away for recycling into neutral spirit.

VAPOUR INFUSION

It's good to visualize the steep and boil process (page 87) as like making a cup of tea. The teabag represents the botanicals, the water the neutral spirit and the aromatic vapour rising off the mug is the gin. But what if the teabag was suspended above the mug, out of contact with the liquid? This is the analogy that I like to use to explain how vapour-infused gins work.

Vapour infusion in gin production was first introduced in the mid-19th century, and first documented in the French distillers' handbook, *Traité des Liqueurs et de la Distillation des Alcools* (1855). Despite what Bombay Sapphire may have you believe, the method was more than likely born out of necessity and convenience rather than flavour innovation.

The introduction of the column still in the 1830s generated a notable leap in spirit quality thanks to its rectifying column and steam-powered design. Other stills were conceived during the era that borrowed elements from the traditional pot and hybridized it with pieces from the column still. One such still was the 'Carter head', designed by a coppersmith of the same name who worked for the renowned still manufacturer John Dore. The Carter head still was simply a pot still heated by a steam jacket with a rectifying column plonked on top. Just like a regular pot still, it could only produce spirit batch after batch, but thanks to the column it could produce a higher strength, purer spirit than with a copper pot.

One of these stills was installed at Bridge Street Distillery in Warrington, England, in 1836. It was a useful piece of kit for purifying low-quality alcohol, but when someone tried to make gin in it they found that the column was too efficient, with the result that the spirit was stripped of all its botanical character. The solution was to attach a sealed drum, fitted with perforated baskets, at the far end of the lynearm. The baskets were filled with gin botanicals, which would infuse into the spirit vapour as it blasted towards the condenser. It worked exceptionally well.

From a distiller's perspective there is one major advantage to distilling this way, and that is the speed of turnaround. In a traditional steep and boil scenario, the distiller has to clean all the cooked botanicals out from the bottom of the pot in between batches, and sometimes a caustic wash is necessary. Refilling and cleaning pots is time-consuming, laborious and messy.

In a still with a vapour infusion chamber, the botanicals never come into contact with the still, or indeed the liquid spirit. The botanical 'magazines' are simply slotted into place and ejected out again once the work is done. The still itself requires little or no cleaning since

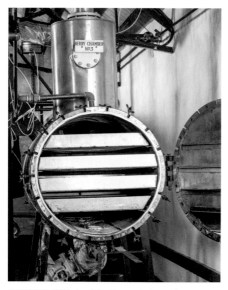

it has only had to deal with ethanol and water, both of which are cleaning products in their own right! Using vapour infusion, a distiller could, in theory, make their tails cut, replace their botanical racks, and recharge the still in a matter of minutes.

ABOVE This 'rack' of botanicals at the Balmenach Distillery features perforated drawers containing each botanical.

DISTILLATION

· ·

With neutral spirit in hand, now it's time to get on with the real gin-making process. As we have already learned, there are various rules that govern how gin can be labelled, and that not all products labelled as gin are as romantically agreeable as we might wish them to be. Here, we delve in to the methods and instruments used to make gin flavour compounds and distilled botanical spirits, as well as the cutting and bottling of gin.

In all instances, gin-making is overseen by the master distiller. In the make-believe distillery wonderland that resides only in your head, this man probably wears a boiler suit and steel toe-capped boots, he has hands like shovels coated in boiled leather and his nose and palate have been honed to a rare state of superhuman sensory perception. I do know of one or two gin distillers that fit that brief, but for the most part the people who make gin are a very diverse bunch, from moustache-toting hipsters, to wizened old gentlemen, with everything in-between. And don't make the mistake of assuming this is only a job for men. Women are proven to have a superior sense of smell over men, and around half a dozen of the distilleries I researched for this book have leading ladies of the drinks business at the helm.

The master distiller's primary responsibility is to produce a quality product and to ensure consistency in the product through continued monitoring and management of the distillation process. Distilling an aromatically desirable product that is both balanced and complex is not as simple as turning on the still, any more than baking a wedding cake is as easy as turning on the oven. An understanding of alcohol and botanicals is essential, but mastering the impact of temperature and vapour pressure in the still and how it impacts flavour extraction and gin composition, along with capturing only the best of the liquid for bottling, is what makes a truly great product.

ABOVE This kind of pot still is common among newer 'craft' distilleries. The spirit can be directed through the central rectifying column if a higher-strength distillate is needed.

LOW-PRESSURE
DISTILLATION

· ·

Low-pressure distillation has its origins in the science lab, where
pieces of equipment like the rotary evaporator (or rotavap) are used
in organic chemistry to split and concentrate liquids with different
boiling points. Put simply, a rotavap is a type of still with a rotating
glass flask that sits in a heated water bath. The pressure of the system
dictates the boiling point of the liquid mixture, and the water bath is
adjusted to meet this. The rotation of the flask increases the surface
area of the liquid mixture and encourages a faster distillation.

Given that the rotavap is a still in its own right, it's ironic that it
has had to travel via kitchens and bars before anyone explored the
possibility of commercially distilling flavoured spirits with one. The
main reasons for this are size and cost. Even a 1-litre (¼-US gallon)
rotavap can easily set you back £5,000 (US$7,400) and the largest
20-litre (5¼-US gallon) set-ups can easily approach six figures.

Crucially, by lowering the boiling point of the liquid, the quantity of
heat-sensitive compounds that may otherwise have been de-natured
or destroyed at traditional temperatures are preserved. Of course,
lower temperatures also mean that some less volatile compounds
that might feature in steep and boil gins might not distil over in
a low-pressure environment. All botanicals contain a complex array
of compounds with differing degrees of volatility. The beauty of
low-pressure distillation is that it allows the distiller to find the ideal
temperature to boil the botanical to showcase the best bits of its
aromatic profile. In general, it's soft and delicate botanicals (flowers,
fresh herbs and fruit) that benefit most from low-pressure, low-
temperature distillation. Hard spices, roots and barks are more
inclined to give up the goods at higher temperatures.

ABOVE Some distilleries use table-top rotary evaporators to distil under low pressure. Others, like Sacred, build a room full of interconnecting glass vessels.

There are two gins in particular that have become synonymous with low-pressure distilling, Sacred and Oxley. The latter uses a one-of-a-kind vacuum still that operates at a near-perfect vacuum. Such a low pressure means that the boiling point of the liquid is below 0°C (32°F), dripping through at around -6°C (21°F). This still requires no heat, since the surrounding atmospheric temperature is enough to trigger the evaporation of the spirit. It does however require significant amounts of energy to run the cooler and vacuum pump.

ONE-SHOT AND MULTI-SHOT

If you hear a gin geek moaning about a 'multi-shot' gin, rest assured that they're not referring to a drinking ritual or an intensive tasting procedure. The topic of 'one-shot' and 'two-shot' (or 'multi-shot') is actually a matter of grave controversy which has resulted in disparity amongst distillers.

One-shot gins are prepared by distilling a given volume of neutral spirit with a given weight of botanicals (page 107). The resulting distillate is then cut down to bottling strength with water and that's the end of the story. With multi-shot gins, which make up the vast majority of the London Dry Gin bottles in your local liquor store, the weight of botanicals is multiplied up, but the quantity of spirit kept the same. The result is a kind of gin concentrate that is then cut back with both neutral spirit and water before being bottled.

The advantages of multi-shot are obvious to see – in a single distillation run you can produce many times the quantity of finished product that can be delivered in a one-shot batch. But those of the one-shot camp see multi-shot as both non-traditional, non-craft and, well – cheating.

The proof is of course in the pudding, and if the blind tastings are anything to go by there's little to tell apart between a cut-back multi-shot and a classic one-shot. Going under the assumption that a still loaded up with botanicals doesn't reach some kind of botanical vapour saturation point, one has to concede that – assuming the maths is correct – a bottle of gin made either way will contain the same quantity of spirit, water and botanical extract in either instance.

ABOVE Gin labels are not legally required to state whether
they're made by a one-shot or multi-shot method.

While we're on this subject, and for what it's worth, I would like
to convey my distaste for the terms 'one-shot' and 'multi-shot'.
They are, in my eyes, both vulgar and inapt, but for reasons
unknown to me they have regrettably become the standard
convention in distillery-speak.

Some common multi-shot gins include: Gordon's, Tanqueray,
Beefeater, Jensen's and anything produced at Langley and Thames.
Some common one-shot gins include: Bombay Sapphire, Sipsmith,
Dodd's, Thomas Dakin and Tarquin's.

COMPOUNDING

Compounding has long been a dirty word in the gin world. And sure enough it's not the most glamorous way to manufacture gin, nor does it require a great deal of artistic flair. A compounder is, by definition, a blender, and that's exactly what's going on here. Individual gin flavours – obtained from sources, natural or unnatural – are mixed with neutral spirit and water to create a product that looks, smells and tastes like gin. And it is gin! According to the law that is. The vast majority of flavoured vodkas are made in the same way, and so too are all the suspicious-looking supermarket own-brands you've seen labelled only as 'gin'. There is no master distiller as such (their title would more likely be master-mixer) and the only skill really lies in the blend's recipe, and its effectiveness at making a chemical cocktail smell and taste like a London Dry Gin.

I viewed compounded gins in this way for many years, but one day an interesting thought occurred to me. If compounded gins are a mixture of concentrated flavours and neutral spirit, isn't that the same as a multi-shot gin? Sure, multi-shots are distilled, but so are a lot of compounded flavour extracts, so how do the two differ?

The truth is that they don't, and the problem here lies in terminology confusing itself with classification. We naturally assume that a compounded gin is not a distilled gin, because the process suggests a degree of corner-cutting and cost-saving. We also take it for granted that a gin brand that speaks of provenance, craft and flavour is a one-shot London Dry. Most of the time these conclusions are valid, but it is absolutely not the case all of the time and it's for this reason that we should refer to the gin's classification (pages 130–139) to better understand its production process before drawing conclusions from the authentic look and feel of the bottle, or some other similarly cunning distraction.

ABOVE Sacks of botanicals are evident at Hendrick's Distillery, but the gin is flavoured with compounded essences, too.

Let's take Sacred and Hendrick's as a pair of examples. Sacred is a made from top-quality botanicals that are individually macerated and distilled into super-concentrated liquids using a home laboratory. These extracts are then sent away to be blended (read: compounded) with a lot of neutral spirit, then cut down with water before bottling. Sacred is a compounded gin, but it is also a London Dry Gin because it adheres to all of the requirements of the classification. Hendrick's, on the other hand, is distilled in a copper pot and packaged in a legitimate fashion, but it also contains cucumber and rose extract that are added after distillation. For this reason it is not a London Dry Gin.

In summary, yes, some – perhaps most – compounded gins are a bit nasty. Mixing one part juniper extract with 1,000 parts neutral spirit will never produce a gin that boasts the aromatic and textural finesse of a copper distilled one-shot product.

CUTTING AND
BOTTLING

The heart of the product, now a high-strength gin of at least 70% (for a London Dry) and possibly as high as 90% ABV, is ready for the next stage of the process.

For a compounded or multi-shot gin, it's time to be cut back with neutral spirit. This is the stage where de-mineralized water is added to dilute the product down to bottling strength.

In the EU, gin has to be a minimum of 37.5% ABV, while for the US it's slightly higher, at 80 proof (40% ABV). Premium gins tend to all be a minimum of 40% ABV and some are much higher. In fact, if you glance over a selection of premium gins you'll probably find that they all differ in strength – 41.4%, 43.7%, 45.2% and so on. This is not a case of more booze means a better product, nor is it a desperate attempt to claim ownership of a specific alcohol content (although some brands do appear to have achieved this).

Gin presents its botanical aroma quite differently depending on the strength of the product. The molecules carrying aroma are more chemically similar to alcohol molecules than water so they tend to latch on to alcohol molecules. This means that a drink that is high in alcoholic strength tends to sequester its aroma molecules away in the liquid of the drink, giving very little away on the aroma side of things. Add some water – a common practice amongst malt whisky drinkers – and suddenly the aroma is revealed. In the case of gin, honing in on a particular ABV can amplify or suppress certain botanical characteristics, allowing the distiller to divulge just the right amount of the drink's aromatic properties.

LEFT AND ABOVE At G&J Distillers in Warrington – the UK's oldest continually operating gin distillery – supermarket gins (left) and super-premium gins (above) are all made and bottled under the same roof. It's a huge operation featuring all sorts of technical wizardry, with only six or so employees needed to check that everything's going to plan.

The irony of all this is, of course, that very few people drink gin straight from the bottle. It's mixed, with either tonic water or in a cocktail, and once mixed all that detail goes out of the window.

Even if you drink gin on ice – and you're really in the minority there – the drink will be diluted, and consequentially its aroma will have been adjusted. Even if you are one of the 20-or-so people in the whole world who drinks neat gin at room temperature, the shape and size of your glass will also have some bearing on aroma perception, too. The point is that, besides the controlled tasting room scenario, the ABV of the product is not particularly important unless it comes with precise instructions explaining how to mix it.

HOW GENEVER IS MADE

Genever production guidelines are vague, so the process differs from one distillery to the next. Unlike gin, which is a botanical distillate sometimes blended with neutral spirit, a bottle of genever comprises at least three components (as well as water) and sometimes many more. Based on the ratio of components, a bottle will labelled as *Oude* (aged), *Jonge* (young), *Corenwijn* (grain wine) and so on, but there's some confusion with these terms, specifically with *Oude* and *Jonge*. Most of us associate 'old' with 'aged', and since many genevers undergo maturation in oak casks, it's an obvious connection to make. However, oak-ageing is not a pre-requisite of the *Oude* style (it is for *Corenwijn*), but it does often happen. A better title for *Oude* and *Jonge* would be 'old-fashioned' and 'new' respectively.

The first and most important of the components is *moutwijn* ('malt wine'), a richly flavoured cereal-based pot-still distillate. The mash of cereals is any combination of rye, corn, wheat and barley, with the ratios dictating character in the finished genever. Of all the malt wine produced in Belgium and The Netherlands, 99% is made by Filliers Distillery who tailor the recipe to their clients' requirements. If wheat and corn are used, they are mixed with water and cooked at a high temperature to loosen up the starch. As the mixture cools, rye is added, followed by barley. If the barley is malted, it releases enzymes that break the cereal's starches down into simple fermentable sugars. Unlike malt whisky production, the law permits the diastase enzyme to be used in its pure form in place of malted barley grain. The sweet, bread-y liquid 'wort' is then drained from the mash and yeast is added to promote fermentation, which converts the sugar into alcohol. This takes 3–7 days and because the speed of the process has a direct impact on flavour, it is tailored to the brand. The fermented mash, or beer, is then stripped of its alcohol in a continuous still, then redistilled two or three times in linked pot-stills. In some distilleries, like Zuidam, the distillation is done entirely in pot stills, giving a fruitier, drier spirit compared to the nutty, cereal notes that come from the column-still method used at Filliers.

If a column is being used, the first spirit will be drawn off at around 48% ABV. After subsequent distillations it may be as high as 80%, but is typically closer to the 70% mark. The first distillate, which comes off the continuous still, is called *ruwnat* ('rough wet'); the second distillate (from the first linked pot-still) *enkelnat* ('single wet'); and the third distillate (from a second linked pot-still) *bestnat* ('best wet'), otherwise known as malt wine. For the optional fourth distillate (from an optional third linked pot-still) you get *korenwijn* ('grain wine'), which should not be confused with the finished product *Korenwijn* (also spelled *Corenwijn/Corenwyn*) (see below). A portion of the malt wine is then re-distilled with juniper and (optionally) other botanicals, like coriander seed, caraway seed or fennel seed. The concentrated *habaida* (berry) *moutwijn* is then blended with unflavoured malt wine. Sometimes a botanical distillate made from neutral spirit is mixed in too.

All genever was made this way until the mid-19th century, but the invention of the continuous still in 1831 changed everything. The availability of cheap, neutral, flavourless spirit gave economically minded genever distillers the option to dilute their flavoursome malt wine and 'stretch' it a lot further. This gave rise to the individual styles of genever that we recognise today: *Moutwijn* (100% malt wine), *Corenwijn* (at least 51% malt wine), *Oude* (15–51% malt wine), and *Jonge* (under 15% malt wine but typically less than 5%).

After malt wine, botanical spirit, and neutral spirit have been mixed, the distiller needs only to add water to achieve the correct bottling strength – this is how all *jonge* genever is made. Alternately, the spirit can be aged in oak casks no bigger than 700 litres (185 US gallons) for a period of no less than one year.

BOTANICALS

Botanicals are an essential component of gin (and genever) production as they give the product its aroma and flavour. Simply put, botanicals are substances obtained from plants, or anything that grows: fruit, seed, root, bark, flower, leaf or grass. The range of options is infinite, and I see this as one of the driving forces behind the revitalization of the gin category as new distillers customize their recipes to a specific profile of flavours.

Generally speaking, gin is made in the same way as an essential oil, where a solvent (in this case alcohol) is heated and the vapour used to carry the volatile aromatic components of the plant. All

ABOVE Once a botanical recipe has been formulated, it's up to each distillery to ensure the quality of these natural ingredients is consistent from batch to batch.

botanicals contain a range of compounds, some of which we can taste and some that we can smell. Molecules that are geared more towards smell (pine, cinnamon or lemon, for example) are much lighter than those we associated with taste, and it's for this reason that we are able to smell them in the first place – they carry to our noses with a greater ease. We describe them as being more 'volatile' – which is apt, since 'volatiles' are interesting, unstable and often elusive.

Gin making is all about extracting a desirable range of these volatile aromatic molecules from a selection of botanicals. In addition to the recipe, the presses used to extract them along with the quantity of botanical used will go on to dictate the style of gin. It gets more interesting when you consider that some gins' most desirable compounds can be present across many different botanicals. The compound *pinene* (which gives gin its sweet, woodsy, pine aroma) for example, is found in juniper, coriander seed, angelica, cinnamon and many other botanicals besides. It's in this manner that, historically, a variety of botanicals were used to bolster the juniper flavour of gin through their own *pinene* content, but also augment it with other, harmonious flavours.

These days things have moved on somewhat and even though many brands stick to the classic juniper-driven style, the options that the world of botany presents us with have led others to experiment with all kinds of weird and wonderful botanical combinations. Over the next few pages we will explore some of the more classic examples.

JUNIPER

The common juniper tree (*Juniperus communis*) is a coniferous plant and a member of the Cupressaceae (cypress) family. It can grow up to 10 m (30 ft) tall and live for over 100 years, but those cultivated for gin production are engineered to be much shorter and bushier. Common juniper has the widest geographical range of any tree in the world, taking up residence in western Alaska, across Canada and northern parts of the USA, in coastal areas of Greenland, Iceland, throughout Europe, north Africa, and in northern Asia and Japan. It's content in either acid or alkaline soils and can be found across a variety of landscapes.

ABOVE A juniper tree overlooks the barren slopes of the Annapurna mountain range of the Himalayas in Nepal.

Juniper is a slow-grower, taking a leisurely 10 years before the plant produces flowers and fruit. Individual plants are either male or female, unlike most tree species, where both male and female flowers occur on the same tree. Male flowers present themselves as yellow blossoms near the ends of the twigs in spring and disperse pollen into the wind. Female flowers look like very small clusters of scales, and after being pollinated, they become tiny cones, which soften and grow into juniper berries.

Shaped like irregularly-sided spheres, juniper berries are green at first, but ripen only after 12–18 months to a dark, blue-purple. They are about 0.5–1 cm (¼–½ inch) in diameter when fresh. Each berry contains 3–6 triangular seeds, which are dispersed by birds that eat the berries. Given that it takes so long for the berries to ripen, it's normal to see ripe and unripe fruit at any one time. This means the same tree may be harvested three times over a two-year period.

Most of the juniper used to make gin is sourced from Italy or Macedonia. Juniper can still be found in the UK, especially Scotland, but the fungus *Phytophthora austrocedrae* has decimated up to 70% of Britain's juniper in recent years and, in general, the tree is at risk of extinction throughout the British Isles. Considering that the industry uses an extraordinary quantity of juniper, it's surprising to find that most juniper trees are not farmed or cultivated and picking is more akin to foraging than harvesting. Traditionally, pickers will circulate around a tree, beating the branches and catching the falling berries in a round flat basket. On a good day,

BELOW LEFT Juniper berries in the first year of their growing cycle, when they are hard and green. BELOW CENTRE Ripe juniper berries, most likely in the second year of their growing cycle. BELOW RIGHT Juniper is usually dried for use in gin production. This takes about 3 weeks, or a few days in a dehydrator.

an experienced beater can collect their own bodyweight in berries.

The earliest recorded medicinal use of juniper dates back to ancient Egypt, around 1500 BC, when the brown coloured fruit of *Juniperus phoenicea* was used as a poultice to treat joint and muscle pain. Athletes in Greece's ancient Olympic Games gobbled up juniper berries, believing they would improve performance. The Romans used juniper for a range of digestive ailments, and famous medieval herbalist Culpepper used juniper infusions for the relief of trapped wind, for which juniper oil is still used today.

The volumes of juniper oil and its constituents can change dramatically according to a berry's ripeness, the age of the plant, period of harvesting and terroir. In general, the essential oil content of juniper cones peaks at around 3% just before the fruit reaches full ripeness. Over 70 different components have been identified in the oil, but it is largely made up of five flavourful compounds called terpenes. Pinene is the main terpene in juniper, and there are no prizes for guessing the aroma that it imparts. There are actually two types of pinene in juniper. Alpha-pinene, the principal of the two, has a woodsy cedar-like aroma. Beta-pinene is found in much smaller quantities, and can be distinguished by a green, Christmas tree-type aroma.

Other important terpenes in juniper are myrcene, which gives a lingering herbal, mossy aroma; sabinene, offering a warm, slightly nutty aroma; and limonene, providing freshness and citrus notes.

CORIANDER

The green leaves of the coriander plant (*Coriandrum sativumis*) are used liberally in some Middle Eastern, Asian and Central American cuisine. North Americans have adopted the Spanish word for coriander leaves – cilantro - due to the plant's habitual use in Mexican cuisine. The leaves and stalks have a highly perfumed, bright, and grassy flavour, and those who dislike coriander/cilantro (approximately 15% of the world) tend to do so vehemently thanks to a genetic predisposition that causes some people to detect a sickly 'soapiness' in the aldehydes present in the plant.

In the production of gin, it is not the leaves that are used, but the seeds – or I should say, fruit. The fruit of the herb tastes quite different to the leaves, as it is dried during preparation, removing much of the vibrant green characteristics of the fresh plant. And it's these perfect little sand-coloured spheres that you will find in the spice section of your local market, as well as your gin. Coriander fruit has a far more diverse range of abilities when compared to the leaves, thanks to a symphony of active flavour compounds

ABOVE Coriander seeds lose their potency very quickly once ground up, so are better stored whole.

that play nicely with other ingredients. The seeds are used extensively in the curry dishes of India (where they are called *dhania*), as a pickling spice for onions and cucumbers, as a sausage spice for the South African *boerewors*, as well as in the production of some citrus wheat beers, herbal liqueurs, and are second only to juniper in gin botanical rankings.

FACT FILE

Typical cost per 10 kg (22 lbs.):
£40 (US$60)

Particularly prevalent in:
Dr. J's, Tanqueray London Dry,
Cremorne 1859.

Flavour profile:
Sweet spice, lemon balm, sage,
cedar, white chocolate, lemon
curd, lemonade, earl grey tea.

Coriander seeds have a distinct lemon aroma, more lemony than lemon itself I would argue. It's coriander seed that contributes the citrus aromas to many of the world's best gins that mysteriously have no lemon or orange zest on their botanical shopping list. The citrus characteristic of coriander can be attributed to the combination of four terpenes: linalool, thymol, pinene and geranyl acetate. Linalool's highly desirable spiced floral aroma is synthesized in huge quantities and is thought to be used in over half of the world's scented cleaning products. Thymol gives us a warm and woody incense; geranyl acetate is floral and feminine; and pinene is found in high concentrations in pine needles and nuts. It is also a major player in juniper, so does a neat job of binding the two botanicals together with a fresh, potent cedar wood aroma.

As with any other botanical, the aromatic profile of the seed will vary according to its specific variety and origin. It's widely accepted that the best coriander seed comes from the *microcarpum* variety. These plants flourish in eastern Europe, Russia and Scandinavia (all places that, ironically, use relatively little coriander in their cuisine) and is famed for its small fruits that pack a big punch. The alternate is the sub-tropical variety, *vulgaris*, which can be found India, parts of Asia and northern Africa.

CARDAMOM

Cardamom is the third most expensive spice in the world after saffron and vanilla, and since those two are scarcely seen in gin, it makes cardamom the most expensive for our purposes. Cardamom is painfully difficult to process, requiring specific quality standards at every stage.

Cardamom is native to Southern India and is grown commercially in its surrounding countries, but today the world's largest grower is Guatemala. Guatemala has the German coffee planter, Oscar Majus Kloeffe, to thank for the 30,000 tons of cardamom they now produce annually – he took cuttings from India and planted them there at the end of the 19th century.

Two genera of cardamom grown commercially for flavouring and both belong to the ginger (Zingiberaceae) family. *Elettaria Cardamomum* is the common green cardamom (also known as true cardamom) and *Amomum cardamomum* is the black (or brown) type. Green cardamom, which can be found in a lot of Indian food and

ABOVE The more vivid the colour of green cardamom, the more it's worth.

medicine is more aromatic, 'greener' and fresh tasting than black, which takes on a spicy, smokey quality useful in Asian cooking. Both pack a serious punch, so only a little is required to reach a desirable effect.

While still on the plant, the pods resemble pale green olives, growing low to the ground and often creep along the ground like a necklace of beads. Once picked, they are washed and dried at exactly 50°C (122°F) for about 6 hours. Stalks are removed and the pods are then graded by

passing the pods through different sized apertures, which aims to weed out underdeveloped or overripe pods. Most often the pods are hand-graded too, where shrivelled or diseased pods are discarded. Quality is paramount and it's not unusual for cardamom to undergo additional screening before being packaged for sale. In India and Sri Lanka the pods are graded in three categories: Alleppey Green Bold (AGB), Aleppey Green Extra Bold (AGEB) and Alleppey Green Superior (AGS). The greener the pods, the more expensive the cardamom is. The pods can then be ground whole, hulled for their seeds, or used whole for gin production.

Both green and black cardamom share a group of terpenes: cienol, which is a major contributor to the fragrance of eucalyptus; and fragrant and fresh terpinyl acetate, the same stuff that can be found in the leaves of some citrus trees and pine oil. Both of these terpenes are found in rosemary and basil, too. What differentiates the two cardamom genera is a healthy measure of the citrus-scented terpene, limonene, in green cardamom, whereas black cardamom favours beta-pinene, giving it a woody, green note.

LIQUORICE

The liquorice/licorice plant (*Glycyrrhiza glabra*) is actually a legume, so, like lentils and peas, it produces a kind of podded fruit. The pods are next to useless, and I haven't found a single reference of anyone using them for anything. It is, of course, the root of the liquorice/licorice plant that gets flavorists excited, valued for its intense sweetness, and earthy anise qualities. Liquorice's/licorice's medicinal uses stretch back as far as medicine itself. Ancient Chinese pharmacists positioned it amongst the highest class of drugs for its adeptness tackling fever, thirst, cough and respiratory ailments. The Ancient Egyptians enjoyed liquorice/licorice recreationally, turning the root into a sweet non-alcoholic drink that must have tasted something like watered-down molasses.

These days, liquorice/licorice is still used medicinally, but can also be found in a wide range of soft drinks, food products and cigarettes. It's been estimated that over half of the world's liquorice/licorice root is used to flavour tobacco products. It would seem that the sweet, earthy flavour of liquorice/licorice does a good job of

ABOVE Liquorice/licorice root is quite expensive, so should never been confused with kindling!

enhancing the flavour of tobacco while softening its harshness. My father was, at one time, a staunch follower of liquorice-/licorice-flavoured papers in his 'roll-up' cigarettes.

Liquorice/licorice root contains a powerful natural sweetener called glycyrrhizin [glis-eer-riz-in], taken from the greek words *gluku* (sweet) and *rrhiza* (root). Glycyrrhizin is a tooth-softening 50 times sweeter than table sugar (sucrose) but before you send lilies to your dentist, know

that much of the brunt of the force is perceived as a lingering sweetness rather than a full frontal assault. Liquorice/licorice root can contain anywhere from 4–25% glycyrrhizin by dry weight, so it can pack a serious sweet punch.

When I worked at the Gordon's Distillery in Cameron Bridge for a day, liquorice/licorice was the only one of the gin's 10 botanicals that was not automatically deposited into the still. This meant bundling a heavy bag (around 10 kg/22 lbs.) of ground liquorice/licorice root through the hatch. I can still remember the sensation of the oleaginous dust fixing to my tongue as I inhaled, turning into a sweet glue on my palate. The flavour stayed with me all day.

Besides fenchone, which is the ketone that gives camphor its distinct aroma, liquorice/licorice root has a hefty dose (around 3% of the dry weight) of the compound anethole. Anethole is a compound that contributes a large part of the 'aniseed' flavour of fennel and anise – plants that belong to the Apiaceae family – and it is the missing link between the aromatic similarities of these plant species and liquorice/licorice.

ORRIS

The *Iris pallida* is native to Croatia's Dalmation coast and is a hardy plant with sword-shaped leaves that produces purple to white flowers. The flower is thought to be the basis of the French 'fleur-de-lys', but it is the root of the plant (or rhizome) that botanists have a greater interest in. The plant has been cultivated for its root since Roman times, which, when dried, is prized for its perfume and its usefulness as a fixative – an odour that assembles and supports other aromas. Today, *I. pallida* is grown in surprisingly small quantities, mainly in Italy and especially in Tuscany – where it is known colloquially as 'giaggiolo' – along with its descendant *I. germanica*

RIGHT AND BELOW With a flower that pretty, it's only fair that *Iris pallida* has an ugly (but brilliantly perfumed) rhizome.

var. Florentina, found in Morocco, China and India, and *I. germanica* '*Albicans*', which is also used in orris production.

Three-year-old plants are proven to provide the best yield of rhizome development, as the rate of growth of the rhizome slows after that period. Harvesting during dry spells is preferred, as the skin of the root tends to fall away naturally due to dehydration. The root is cut from the leafy plant, and the plant is

then inserted back into the ground where it grows fresh roots. The root itself is washed, peeled and dried. Because there's less than 80 hectares (200 acres) of commercially grown orris in the world, this process is generally very hands-on. Also, it takes almost 1 metric ton of orris root to make 2 litres/½ US gallon of orris essential oil (known as orris butter).

The fresh roots smell of little more than earth. The development of desirable floral characteristics is only possible through a drying period of up to five years, which sees some of the root's duller constituents oxidize into a group of closely related aromatic compounds called irones and ionones. Orris's unique combination of irones and ionones results in a complex floral and woody quality that is as prized amongst perfumers and gin manufacturers as it is expensive – a reflection of orris's lengthy preparation process.

CINNAMON & CASSIA

Cinnamon and cassia are commonly confused with one another, and in North America especially, there are a great deal of products sold as cinnamon that are in fact cassia. Although both belong to the Lauraceae family and the *Cinnamomum* genus, cinnamon and cassia do not come from the same plant. Both are harvested in a similar manner, however, wherein strips of inner bark in young trees are dried in the sun and rolled into the familiar sticks of spice.

The *Cinnamomum* genus has over 300 species, but scientifically speaking, there is only one true cinnamon. Commonly known as Ceylon cinnamon, named for the fact that it is found almost exclusively in Sri Lanka, it comes from the *Cinnamomum verum*

ABOVE LEFT These quills are recognizable as cassia because of their hollow, brittle structure. ABOVE RIGHT All of the world's cassia and cinnamon is still stripped and rolled by hand.

plant, which literally translates as 'true cinnamon'. This stuff is the Champagne of the cinnamon world and the rolled quills of its highly aromatic bark are distinguishable by numerous layers of soft, thin, velvet-textured wafers.

Cinnamomum cassia (also known as *C. aromaticum*) is more like the Pinot Grigio of tree bark spices. It's readily available and passable. Most of the world's cassia heralds from China (it's also known as Chinese cinnamon) and Vietnam, but it is grown widely across Southeast Asia and Madagascar. Cassia takes its name from the Hebrew word *qãtsa*, meaning 'to strip off bark'. If you look at the cross-section of a cassia quill, you will see that only one or two thick layers of bark make up the furl.

The aromatic oils of cinnamon trees are used extensively to flavour meat and in fast-food seasonings, sauces and pickles, baked goods, confectionery, soft drinks, tobacco flavours and in dental and pharmaceutical preparations. They are also used to flavour a number of spirits and liqueurs.

Most gins opt for cassia, and even most of those gins that state they are using cinnamon are in fact sourcing it from cassia trees in China or Vietnam. There are a few exceptions to the rule, however. Sipsmith use both cassia, from China, and true cinnamon, from Madagascar in their gin recipe.

ABOVE Cinnamon trees are harvested in the wet season when the bark is softer.

That familiar cinnamon flavour comes from the flavour compound cinnamaldehyde. Ceylon cinnamon trumps cassia in the cinnamaldehyde stakes, but the lesser known Saigon cinnamon (*C. loureiroi*), which is grown exclusively in Vietnam, beats them both. It can contain up to 3% essential oil by dry weight, of which over 80% is cinnamaldehyde. Other compounds consistent to all cinnamon species are pinene, linalool, limonene and camphene – all familiar names (see pages 109–115).

The flavour that cassia contributes to gin is somewhat spicier than the soft and round flavour that you might associate with cinnamon, mostly thanks to a terpene called alpha-guaiene, which brings a woody heat to the product. But I believe that slightly spicy botanicals like cassia can have the effect of softening the alcohol burn in the finished product, whereby the presence of a cinnamon aroma justifies a slight burn where it would otherwise be austere or unexpected. In other words, the burn becomes acceptable because the flavour permits it.

ANGELICA

Angelica belongs to the Apiacae (carrot) family of hollow-stem aromatic shrubs, making it a cousin of coriander, anise, fennel, dill, celery and parsnip – to name but a few. There are over 60 known species of angelica. Some, like *Angelica sinensis* (Dong Quai), are used in Chinese cooking and medicine, while others are indigenous to Europe and the West coast of the US. The Eurasian species of angelica, *Angelica archangelica*, is the one that we are interested in.

A. Archangelica takes its name from the Greek word *arkhangelos* after the myth that it was first introduced to mankind by the Archangel Gabriel. The plant flourishes across Scandinavia, where it stands as a respected medicinal herb used to treat respiratory ailments, and as a digestive aid since as far back as the 10th century. It also features in the traditional cuisine of Iceland and the Faroe Islands, where it is known as *hvonn* and is consumed like a vegetable. Its uses were not limited to the physical either; in the Middle Ages it was common for children to wear angelica-leaf necklaces to ward off evil spirits and it was widely believed that witches gave it a wide berth.

In 17th century *arkhangelos* was required to live up to its name. The bubonic plague was taking its toll on Europe's population

ABOVE Angelica is one of the most important but least understood gin botanicals.

and it was claimed that chewing on the plant helped ward off the plague. This, in turn, meant the countryside in Britain was stripped almost entirely of angelica. If you're thinking about foraging your own, you should be very careful because the plant is very similar in appearance to water hemlock, which possesses a deadly cicutoxin.

These days, the stem of the plant, which looks a lot like a stick/rib of celery (*A. archangelica* is also known as wild celery), is sometimes candied into a baton of sickly-sweet acid-green mulch that's widely used to decorate cakes and flavour puddings – although it's somewhat less fashionable than it might have been thirty years ago. The tiny fruits (seeds) of the plant are sometimes used to flavour absinthe and occasionally crop up in gin, too.

It's the angelica root that we are mostly interested in, however. When dried, the root has a wonderful herb and musk character to it and when brewed into a tea, can be used medicinally. It's for this reason that it crops up in many, if not *most*, of the better known herbal liqueurs, *amari* and bitters,

ABOVE Dried angelica root is visually indistinguishable from any other dried root. It tastes quite root-y too.

ABOVE Angelica grows in the wild in many parts of the UK, but should not be confused with similar-looking water hemlock or cow parsley.

including Chartreuse, Benedictine, Fernet and Galliano. The roots are harvested while the plant is still young and tender, typically in its first year, before it even has a chance to seed a new generation.

I've always been told that angelica's role in gin is to bind the other botanicals together, rather than contribute an original flavour of its own. Indeed, angelica is on the inventory of every single gin containing at least four botanicals. By itself, the root tastes generically herbal and warming to me – much like the aroma of a health food store. That

ABOVE Angelica stems are perfect for being candied or for brewing a sweet, peppery tea.

green, herbaceous note comes partly from a terpene called phellandrene, which, when isolated, has a peppery, minty and slightly citrusy aroma. Couple that with limonene (lemon oil) and our old friend pinene (pine) and you have a botanical that fits into the gin family rather nicely. Having said that, in this author's opinion, angelica root doesn't taste wildly different to other aromatic roots, like orris, burdock and dandelion. I'd like to see the latter two used more in gin production.

LIGHT

FLAVOUR MAP

This chart shows a selection of gins I have tasted and where they sit in terms of style and depth of flavour. 'Classic' gins include more traditional juniper-forward offerings, whereas 'contemporary' gins may lead with citric flavours or focus on unconventional ingredients.

GREENALL'S ORIGINAL LONDON DRY
37.5% ABV

JUNIPER GREEN
37.5% ABV

BOMBAY SAPPHIRE
40% ABV

BEEFEATER 24
45% ABV

BOMBAY EAST
42% ABV

PLYMOUTH
41.2% ABV

GORDON'S LONDON DRY
47% ABV

CITADELLE
44% ABV

BOMBAY ORIGINAL
37.5% ABV

EAST LONDON LIQUOR CO. LONDON DRY
40% ABV

CAORUNN
41.8% ABV

STAR OF BOMBAY
47.5% ABV

BEEFEATER LONDON DRY
40% ABV

WARNER EDWARDS HARRINGTON DRY
44% ABV

TARQUIN'S
42% ABV

FORD'S
45% ABV

ZUIDAM DUTCH COURAGE DRY GIN
44.5% ABV

SIPSMITH
41.6% ABV

PORTOBELLO ROAD NO. 171
42% ABV

TANQUERAY LONDON DRY
43.1% ABV

QUININE 1897
45.8% ABV

RUTTE DRY GIN
35% ABV

HAYMAN'S LONDON DRY
40% ABV

BURLEIGH'S
40% ABV

OLD RAJ
55% ABV

PICKERING'S
42% ABV

FINSBURY PLATINUM
47% ABV

CREAM
43.8% ABV

JENSEN'S BERMONDSEY DRY
43% ABV

DOROTHY PARKER
44% ABV

SIPSMITH VJOP
57% ABV

G'VINE NOUAISON
43.9% ABV

HEPPLE
45% ABV

BURLEIGH;S DISTILLER'S CUT
47% ABV

FIFTY POUNDS
43.5% ABV

HAYMAN'S OLD TOM
40% ABV

DODD'S
49.9% ABV

HAYMAN'S ROYAL DOCK
57% ABV

PERRY'S TOT
57% ABV p.181

HERNÖ SWEDISH EXCELLENCE
40.5% ABV

MARTIN MILLER'S
40% ABV

GIN DE MAHÓN
38% ABV

PROFESSOR CORNELIUS AMPLEFORTH'S BATHTUB NAVY STRENGTH
57% ABV

MARTIN MILLER'S WESTBOURNE STRENGTH
45.2% ABV

SILENT POOL
43% ABV

BROKER'S
47% ABV

JENSEN'S OLD TOM
43% ABV

THE LAKES
43.7% ABV

WILLIAMS CHASE GREAT BRITISH EXTRA DRY
40% ABV

OLD ENGLISH GIN
44% ABV

HEAVY

CLASSIC

LIGHT

CONTEMPORARY

BLOOM
40% ABV

SACRED
40% ABV

OXLEY
47% ABV

FILLIERS DRY GIN 28
46% ABV

HENDRICK'S
41.4% ABV

GILPIN'S WESTMORLAND
EXTRA DRY
47% ABV

THE BOTANIST
46% ABV

AVIATION
42% ABV

DEATH'S DOOR
47% ABV

EDEN MILL ORIGINAL
42% ABV

G'VINE FLORAISON
40% ABV

GIN MARE
42.7% ABV

WHITLEY NEILL
42% ABV

ST. GEORGE BOTANIVORE
45% ABV

EAST LONDON LIQUOR CO.
BATCH NO. 2
47% ABV

DARNLEY'S VIEW
40% ABV

ST. GEORGE TERROIR
45% ABV

THOMAS DAKIN
42% ABV

WILLIAMS CHASE
EUREKA CITRUS GIN
40% ABV

TANQUERAY NO. TEN
47.3% ABV

BERKELEY SQUARE
40% ABV

MONKEY 47
47% ABV

PICKERING'S 1947
42% ABV

EDINBURGH GIN
43% ABV

LANGLEY'S NO.8
41.7% ABV

FEW AMERICAN GIN
40% ABV

NOLET'S DRY GIN
'SILVER
47.6% ABV

HALF HITCH
40% ABV

WILLIAMS CHASE
ELEGANCE 'CRISP'
48% ABV

ADNAM'S COPPER HOUSE
40% ABV

ZUIDAM DUTCH COURAGE
OLD TOM'S
40% ABV

PROFESSOR
CORNELIUS
AMPLEFORTH'S
BATHTUB GIN
43.3% ABV

ADNAM'S FIRST RATE
48% ABV

OPIHR
40% ABV

NOLET'S RESERVE
52.5% ABV

HEAVY

CLASSIFICAION

Before we tackle the complexities of production, it's sensible to first define what gin and juniper-flavoured spirits actually are. Fortunately for us, the rules that govern gin labelling are set out by the European Union, first in 1989 then updated in 2008 to the current Spirit and Drink Regulation, snappily titled '*110/2008*'. Similar regulations are set out in the US (1991), Canada (1993) and Australia (1987), and it's these that we work from today.

JUNIPER-FLAVOURED SPIRIT DRINKS

The most general and non-specific of all the categories of juniper drinks, think of this as the placeholder within which all other categories sit. Over the coming pages, we will explore in detail the two major players within this group: gin and genever.

Any product labelled 'Juniper-Flavoured Spirit Drink' must be a minimum of 30% alcohol by volume (ABV) and it must have a discernible flavour of juniper. Besides that you can do pretty much whatever you want: colourings, sugar, flavourings (artificial or natural) – take your pick.

GIN

It's surprisingly easy to make and sell a product called 'gin'. Only one minor variation on the rules distinguishes a *gin* from a *juniper-flavoured spirit drink*, and that is the strength. In Europe gin must be a minimum of 37.5% ABV (40% for the US).

The rest of the rules remain unchanged; it must contain juniper flavour – be it from natural sources or otherwise – and juniper must be the predominant taste. The latter is a grey area to say the least, as taste is a subjective matter. There are a growing number of juniper-

deficient products that are merrily marketing themselves as gin
and indeed, *London Dry Gin* (page 132). Many of these products are
delicious citrus, spicy or herbal-tasting spirits. But are they gins?
According to the law, no. But since there's no 'gin gestapo' out there
kicking down doors, those brands will no doubt carry on with
business regardless. I don't blame them for wanting to create a great
product that doesn't taste predominantly of juniper, but perhaps a
new category of gin is required to house these renegades (see New
Western Dry Gin, page 136).

So gin is a loose term. You can add colouring, artificial flavouring
and as much sugar as you like. In short, you could walk into your
local liquor store, buy a bottle of vodka and chuck some juniper
berries in it and by the time you get home you would be well
within your rights to legally market it as gin – in fact, it'll probably
taste better than some of the other products out there calling
themselves gin.

DISTILLED GIN

Distilled gin, as set out by the EU, is a gin with one significant
difference: it has to be made using distilled botanicals. Now, what
that means in practical terms is that the juniper element of the gin,
as a bare minimum, must be re-distilled ('re' because the neutral
spirit will have already been distilled at least once) in neutral spirit
of a starting strength of at least 96% and water.

This appears to be good news then, right? Wrong. Rules are made
to be bent, and there would be nothing to stop me distilling two
or three juniper berries in some neutral spirit, and then diluting it
with more spirit, water, sugar, colourings and natural or artificial
flavourings *including* juniper. Revelations such as this do generate
distrust in gins labels as such, but on the flip side of the coin we
have respected brands like Hendrick's and Martin Miller's, which
both sit in the *Distilled Gin* family because both products have
additional flavours added after distillation.

The truth is that some brands packaged as 'Distilled Gin' will be stretching the concept of what a gin should be, but they will remain a *Distilled Gin* nonetheless. Others will be 99% adherents to the *London Dry* classification (see below) but refinements to their process grant them a 'demotion' to the lower league. My opinion is that without more specific definitions, this entire category is rendered a little bit worthless.

OLD TOM

Old Tom is the oldest style of English gin still in production. It is not recognised by the European Union, so it comes with no directions on how to make it. In fact, you could bottle and sell a product called 'Old Tom' bearing no resemblance to gin whatsoever and nobody could do a damn thing about it. But in the hearts and minds of bartenders, Old Tom is hallowed liquid, present at the birth of some of the world's best-loved cocktails and interspersed among the pages of the great cocktail books of the past 150 years. Of the few examples of Old Tom currently in production, all of them generally follow a sweeter path, either through the liberal use of sweet botanicals and/or the addition of sugar.

LONDON DRY

Finally we arrive at a gin definition that can be trusted. Well, except for the London bit that is, because the designation is not geographical and London Dry can in fact be made anywhere in the world. At one time the confusion around where London Dry Gins were made was a bug-bear for some distilleries (unsurprisingly for those based in London), but for the most part the industry has gotten over this terminological entanglement, mostly because those sitting at the discerning end of the table are aware that London Dry has little to do with the city of London.

The London Dry style became popular in London shortly after the column still (also called the continuous still) was invented,

ABOVE It's becoming more common to find gins that list their full botanical array on the bottle. This (along with this book of course!) is your best guide to gin flavour.

RIGHT Some distilleries, like Jensen's, produce more than one style of gin.

eventually replacing Old Tom as the dominant style. The purer spirit that the continuous still offered made a cleaner gin, which could be sold unsweetened, hence the 'dry'. While sugar is desirable in many mixed drinks and cocktails, it is, or at least was, an expensive route to make something taste palatable. If you could get away with not adding it, either because your product was good enough without it or because your target market were too drunk to care, you would have done. Sugar also takes its toll on the drinker, cloying up on the palate and softening the teeth. When the end goal is total and absolute inebriation, it's the dry spirit that will get you there faster.

But London Dry is an important destination in gin production, requiring more rigorous procedure and guaranteeing some degree of proficiency in the gin's production. London Dry Gin follows all the same rules as *Distilled Gin* but must be flavoured exclusively with distilled, natural botanicals. No additional flavourings can be added after the distillation process – in fact nothing at all can be added except for neutral spirit, water and a maximum of 0.1 g sugar per litre.

PLYMOUTH GIN

A category and appellation all of its very own. Or it was, at least. Until 2015, Plymouth Gin was legally bound to be made in Plymouth, Devon, using water from Dartmoor. Since there are no other gins being produced in Plymouth, the gin produced at the Plymouth's Blackfriars Distillery was the only gin in the UK with a geographical indication (GI). This changed in February 2015 however as, somewhat regrettably, this old and outdated classification lost its protected status.

Although driven by the European Union, the decision to withdraw support for the appellation came from Plymouth Gin themselves, who had until February 2015 to submit a dossier outlining the 'particular geographical and organoleptic characteristics' of their product, and they didn't.

On the face of it, the GI seems a harmless relic of the past and a unique selling point for the Plymouth Gin brand, so the motives behind dropping it are not entirely clear. That is, until you consider how circumstances might play out if a brand new distillery opened in Plymouth, declaring compliance to the Plymouth appellation, and demanding a share of the GI-pie – a scenario that could be detrimental to the sales and marketing clout of the existing brand. Unfortunately it's already too late now for that storyline to play out.

One final thought on this matter: the fame and prestige that the GI confers upon Plymouth could also be seen as a prison cell. Giving the GI the heave-ho grants Plymouth gin the ability to distil their product anywhere they like, using any water they like, in the future.

OTHER GEOGRAPHICALLY INDICATED JUNIPER SPIRITS

The European Union currently recognizes 18 juniper-flavoured spirits that are protected by GI. Around half of these are types of genever from The Netherlands, Belgium, France and Germany. The rest can be loosely classed as gins, or juniper brandies, from Spain, Lithuania, Germany and Slovakia.

Gin de Mahón is not a well known style of gin, but it is perhaps the best known of these outlying examples. Originating from the Spanish island of Minorca, Gin de Mahón must be made in the island's capital city, Mahón. Only one brand, Xoriguer (*sho-ri-gair*), is currently protected by this status and it traces its history back to the 18th century. Minorcan gin hasn't made much of an impact internationally, but it certainly makes its mark if you happen to be holidaying on the island. Xoriguer is made in a wood-fired still from eau de vie (wine-based spirit) and locally sourced juniper, then rested in used American oak barrels before bottling.

Vilnius Gin (Vilniaus Džinas) comes from the Lithuanian capital of Vilnius. Vilnius is the only gin currently brandishing the Vilnius

Gin byline, and how and why the city of Vilnius was granted protected status I'm not entirely sure. The Vilnius Gin brand is only 30 years old, a mere pup compared to the likes of Plymouth and Xoriguer, so it seems unlikely that any other product will be jumping at the chance to share the GI any time soon. Vilnius meets all the requirements of a London Dry, and is made using juniper, dill seed, coriander seed and orange peel, to name but a few of its botanicals.

Steinhäger is a type of German gin originating in the Westphalian municipality of Steinhägen, the only place where it is permitted to be produced. In this instance there's a credible claim for the GI, on account of a long history of distilling juniper waters and essential oils in the town. Over 20 distilleries were founded in Steinhägen during the 19th century and two of them still produce Steinhäger gin today: H. W. Schlichte, established in 1766, and Zum Fürstenhof, the latecomer, which was founded in the city of Detmold, in 1902, then moved to Steinhägen in 1955.

The H. W. Schlichte brand markets four types of *Steinhäger* or Juniper Schnapps (as they call it), the most interesting of which is the original Schlichte Steinhäger. Bottled in a genever-style stone crock, this product is not just distilled with juniper berries, but made from spirit that has itself been distilled from 15% ABV fermented juniper berry wine. You don't get much more juniper-y than that!

Finally there is Borovicka, which is a Slovakian style of juniper spirit, similar to dry gin. Only Slovakia can produce Borovicka and there are various regions and types.

'NEW WESTERN DRY GIN'

New Western is an inexact term championed by some contemporary gin producers, especially in the US. It is not a legally recognized category of gin but more of a distinction between the old boy network of London Dry Gins – I'm looking at you Tanqueray and Beefeater – and the current set of citrus, spice, herbal and floral-driven gins that flout the law by allowing other botanicals to share centre-stage with juniper.

If a classification such as New Western Dry was to be put in to effect, its benefit would be two-fold. Firstly, it would create a home for the growing number of interesting and – by their very nature – innovative gins that have forgone the traditional approach. And secondly, it would tighten up the London Dry category, providing sanctuary to only those brands that are faithful to the [juniper] cause. Ultimately it would be the consumer that benefits, allowing them to make a more informed brand choice at the point of purchase, which is the whole point of product labelling in the first place, right?

GENEVER

For those of you who are just beginning to explore the world of Genever (also called Jenever, Geneva, Genebra, Holland(s) Gin, or Dutch Gin), the apparent complexity of the category, as well as potential for pronunciation pitfalls, can make it feel like quite daunting subject matter at first. And truth be told it often is. This is not least down to the fact that there's very little clear-cut law governing how the stuff should be made. In fact, according to the law, Genever need only be produced in either The Netherlands, Belgium, or certain parts of France and Germany – it doesn't even need to be alcoholic!

And that goes for the individual styles of *Jonge* (young), *Oude* (old), and *Korenwijn* (grain wine) too, which are limited only by the location of their production. The manner in which they are made is uniquely constrained by tradition and unwritten law alone, and it's for this reason that I'm using the word 'should' in place of 'must' in the following descriptions. See pages 105–106 for a more detailed look at the production process of Genever.

ABOVE Bols' flagship genever doesn't advertise its style,
but a high maltwine content places it in corenwyn territory.

Jonge Genever, the newer style, is the closest style of genever to London Dry Gin. It is made from neutral spirit and juniper (distilled or otherwise). Other optional flavourings can be added too, it can also contain sugar up to a limit of 10 g (⅓ oz.) per litre/¼ US gallon and it can comprise up to 15% *moutwijn* (malt wine). Since neutral spirit (pages 85–86) can be made from any agricultural source, some products choose to label themselves as *Graanjenever*, indicating that it is made entirely from cereals and not molasses or other sugar products.

Oude genever, the older style, should be made with 15–50% *moutwijn* with the remainder being juniper, other (optional) botanical flavourings, sugar (up to 20 g (⅔ oz.) per litre/¼ US gallon) and neutral spirit. Colourings are also permitted and the product can be matured in oak casks, too, if you like.

Korenwijn, is an even more old-fashioned style of Genever than *Oude* and it is made from 51–70% *moutwijn*. *Korenwijn* is more commonly aged in oak than the other two styles, and its tough flavour profile, which moves closer in style to a whisky than a gin, lends itself well to the softening effects of wood. As with Oude Genever, up to 20 g (⅔ oz.) per litre/¼ US gallon of sugar is permitted.

GIN COCKTAILS

DRY MARTINI

45 ML/1½ FL. OZ. TANQUERAY TEN
10 ML/⅓ FL. OZ. DOLIN DRY VERMOUTH

Add the ingredients to a chilled mixing beaker (kept in the freezer) and stir with lots of cubed ice for at least 90 seconds. Strain into a chilled Martini glass or coupe to serve.

This makes quite a small drink. It's far better, in my opinion, to keep things civilized and keep the Martinis cold. It shouldn't take more than five minutes to drink it in its entirety, which gives you plenty of time to make another round.

A perfect union of two ingredients in any context – food, drink or otherwise – is a thing worth celebrating. Where the Martini is concerned it would appear that we have achieved just that. The cultural significance of this drink is something that most people are aware of, but the true genius of its making is the preserve of a lucky few. A good Martini is potent, but subtle; complex, but clean; cool, but spicy. Most importantly, perhaps, is the beauty that can be found in its brevity. A Martini cannot (and should not) be savoured if it is to be enjoyed properly. It's an all-or-nothing affair. Get stuck in quickly, or lose forever that fleeting chill which softens alcohol, crisps up citrus, and consorts to thicken the texture of the drink on the palate.

The history of this drink is a confusing and often contradictory mess. Essentially, the Dry Martini is a riff on the Martini, which first made its appearance in the 1890s. The Martini was itself nearly identical to the Martinez cocktail, the name having likely been changed to indicate the Martini brand of vermouth that was being used to make the cocktail at the time. Cocktail books from the

late 19th century seldom list both the Martini and Martinez, which leads many of us to conclude that they were Siamese twins of sorts – different names but put together the same way. The Martinez of 1884 was effectively a gin-based Manhattan consisting of two parts Italian vermouth to one part Old Tom gin, bitters and a splash of sugar syrup. The Martinis that landed during the 1890s were the same, most of them made with sweet vermouth and Old Tom gin.

Other drinks from around that time toyed with the idea of dry gin and French (dry) vermouth. The 'Marguerite', published in 1904 called specifically for Plymouth gin, which was mixed with equal parts French vermouth, orange curaçao and orange bitters. Then there was the Turf Club (first appearing in the 1880s) which opted for sweet vermouth, and Harry Johnson's 'Martine' cocktail, which could have been a misspelling of either Martini or Martinez! The world had to wait until the early 1900s for a Dry Martini recognisable by today's standards; Bill Boothby's *The World's The Drinks and How to Mix Them* (1908) calls for equal parts French Vermouth and 'dry English Gin', orange bitters, and to garnish with a squeeze of lemon peel and an olive. There are other references to the drink before Boothby's book, but his is the first I can find that uses French vermouth and dry gin after the modern fashion. Boothby also includes a recipe for a 'Gibson', which is the same drink but without the bitters. Interestingly, we now call a Dry Martini garnished with a silverskin onion a 'Gibson', but Boothby opted for the olive.

Even Boothby's Dry Martini wasn't all that 'dry' when compared with what was to come. The gradual nudging of ratios between gin and vermouth meant that the drink became stronger and less sweet as time went on. As the Martini reached peak dryness in the 1950s – where the slightest glance at a bottle of vermouth, or as Churchill liked to put it, 'a phone-call to France', would suffice – its cold-blooded disposition was the perfect test of a hard-nosed businessman's resolve. Three-martini lunch, anyone? You bet.

As vodka took over, gin died out, and conservative tastes moved on, too. But far from being ignored, the Martini was brought back to life (kicking and screaming) in the 1980s when any drink served in a Martini glass was called an '*insert flavour here* Martini' – ironically, the only things that tended to be absent from the glass were gin and vermouth!

With cocktail culture now firmly back on track, bartenders have revisited the Martini story and paid homage to this, the holiest of all cocktails. I have spent much time mulling over the multitude of variables that make this seemingly simple drink so frustratingly difficult to get right. The truth is that there's a perfect Martini out there for everyone; the difficulty is fathoming out what's right for you. It's probably for this reason that the Martini has stood the test of time. It's more of a concept than a drink in its own right, primed and ready for customization to each drinker's requirements. Ask a bartender to make you a Martini and you should have at least five questions fired back at you. Walk away if you don't.

Here are but a few of my own observations that I think are worth sharing with you. Take them as you will, as they are not gospel, but merely an insight from someone who, over the years, has imbibed and deliberated over their share of Martinis.

Don't assume that drier is better; for me the sweet spot is somewhere between 3:1 and 6:1 in favour of the gin. Use dry ice cubes (i.e. preferably straight from the freezer), otherwise the drink becomes too diluted and a bit flabby. Do dilute the drink enough; a Martini shouldn't be a chore to get through. Martinis generally need stirring for 90 seconds to reach the best possible temperature, and dilution is a part of that process. It's surprisingly difficult to over-dilute a Martini by stirring too long, so take your time. Shaking is fine if you like it that way and it's certainly a lot quicker. Don't go crazy with the garnish. I think it's debatable whether a Martini needs a garnish at all, but a very small piece of lemon peel or an olive is fine.

GIN &
HOMEMADE TONIC

TONIC SYRUP

1 LITRE/34 FL. OZ. WATER

60 G/2 OZ. FINELY GROUND CINCHONA BARK

30 G/1 OZ. GRAPEFRUIT ZEST

3 G/⅛ OZ. GROUND ALLSPICE BERRIES

3 G/⅛ OZ. PINK PEPPERCORNS

15 G/½ OZ. CITRIC ACID POWDER

3 G/⅛ OZ. SALT

1 KG/4 CUPS SUGAR

100 ML/3½ FL. OZ. VODKA

Makes 2 litres/½ US gallon – enough for 40 G&Ts

Place the water, cinchona, zest, ground allspice and peppercorns in a pressure cooker, seal and heat to maximum pressure according to the manufacturer's instructions. After 20 minutes, allow the pressure to release, then strain the liquid through muslin/cheesecloth, removing as much sediment as possible. Let the liquid rest in the fridge for 6 hours, then pour into a clean saucepan, discarding any insoluble matter. Gently heat the infusion and add the citric acid, salt and sugar. When the liquid clarifies, remove from the heat. Finally, add the vodka (it isn't essential, but will double the lifespan of the syrup).

To make your Gin & Tonic, I recommend equal parts of gin and tonic syrup, topped up with a splash of soda and plenty of ice.

There was a time, believe it or not, when a bar call for a G&T would have had heads turning. I cite that period as being between 1970 and 1990, although I'm happy to have my authority questioned since I was either not alive or not of legal drinking age throughout that period. For two decades (give or take), the gin and tonic was a well-kept secret, safeguarded mostly by ladies of a certain age, who opted for refreshment and flavour over a natural compulsion to eschew the beverage that had filled their parents' highballs.

For me, the G&T works thanks to the balance of bitter and sweet. Many of the botanicals found in gin are inherently bitter and some, namely juniper and liquorice/licorice, have a good helping of sweetness, too. But the distillation process neglects to include most of these compounds in the final bottle – physics disallows it. So when bittersweet tonic is mixed with gin, it is like a coming of age or a rediscovery of old values. Throw some bubbles in there too and you have a buoyant, prickly heat that penetrates the tongue with all the aforementioned aromatic and taste qualities. Spices are restored, roots rekindled and fruits and herbs reanimated to their original form. In some respects you could argue that gin is an incomplete package without tonic water – neither product reaching their full potential until mixed with the other.

I've been making tonic water for over a decade and first tried my hand at it while working at Jamie Oliver's Fifteen restaurant, back in 2005. This was before the G&T revolution had gathered pace, and I'm not ashamed to say that we approached the task with a degree of irony. Today, there are over 50 varieties of tonic water available across Europe and the US. That's about 48 more than when I became a bartender. When matched with the grand multiplicity of gins that are now around, the number of unique Gin & Tonics that can potentially be mixed reaches into the tens of thousands.

The tonic must be bittersweet and the gin must be aromatic and in most cases taste of juniper and citrus. Beyond that, the extremities of style within the two categories can result in some very disparate drinks. Take Hendrick's, Aviation or G-Vine Floraison and mix it with Fever Tree Elderflower Tonic Water and you will have a gently floral, softly sweet drink that cowers under the concentrated force of Gin de Mahón or Sipsmith VJOP mixed with Schweppes Tonic.

Quinine, the bitter element of tonic water, can be found in the bark of the cinchona tree. In fact, cinchona remains the only economically practical means of sourcing quinine naturally, and since the synthesis of quinine has proven to be quite tricky, nearly all of the world's quinine still comes from cinchona.

I found it difficult to buy cinchona bark back in 2005, but stumbled across an online source that specialized in herbs and spices for witchcraft! We ground the red bark into a fine powder, then heated it with water to extract the quinine. This was then sweetened and taste-tested. Since we had no real means of measuring the quinine levels - which can be dangerous in high doses - we gauged the right strength based on taste alone, attempting to match the bitterness with Schweppes' offering. A succession of prototype tonics followed, until we finally concocted the finished product. I now use a pressure cooker for the cinchona extraction, as this extracts more of the bitterness and makes the bark go further. It's not essential, but you may need to use more cinchona than stated to get similar levels of bitterness.

Finally, quinine levels do seem to vary from one batch of bark to the next, and like any natural product the tree and its constituents are subject to the whims of terroir and climate. Remember this, and always err on the side of caution when it comes to developing your recipe. As a general rule, bitter things tend to be dangerous and in large enough doses, quinine is no exception. In fact there is a medical condition unique to quinine, known as cinchonism, characterized by a ringing in the ears, headache, abdominal pain and sweating. In the US, the Food and Drug Administration (FDA) regulates tonic water and permits no more than 85 parts of quinine per million, which works out as 0.0085% quinine. If in doubt, send your tonic water off to a food-testing lab to have its quinine levels analysed.

WHIPPER GIN FIZZ

200 ML/7 FL. OZ. GIN (TRY AN OLD TOM)
350 ML/12 FL. OZ. MINERAL (BOTTLED) WATER
110 ML/12 FL. OZ. LEMON JUICE (PULP REMOVED)
60 ML/2 OZ. SUGAR SYRUP (MADE WITH
2 PARTS SUGAR TO 1 PART WATER)
30 G/1 OZ. EGG WHITE

Makes 750 ml/25 fl. oz./3 cups, or approx. 6 small serves

Mix all the ingredients together thoroughly in a large jug/pitcher or blender. Pour carefully into a 1-litre (34-fl. oz) soda siphon (adjust the recipe proportionately for smaller or larger siphons) and place in an iced water bath for an hour.

Once fully chilled, charge the siphon once with carbon dioxide (CO_2). Once charged, shake the siphon, then turn upside-down and release a blast of gas. Charge again, shake, then put it back on ice for five minutes. Shake again before dispensing into ice-cold highball glasses.

There a number of ways to pimp this drink. A pinch of salt goes down a treat, as does a splash of olive oil and a dot of good-quality vanilla extract.

One of the marks of a truly great cocktail is resilience, and I mean that in two senses. Firstly, that the drink is abiding in its design, capable of merrily riding out trends and leading the charge in better times. Secondly, the drink must be resistant to creative hazards. Whether dressed up with exotic ingredients or festooned with an elaborate garnish, the conceptual standards of the cocktail must remain in place at all times. The Martini failed in the latter, having been bastardized beyond all recognition. The Margarita is a good example of a drink that has aged quite gracefully, but there is perhaps no other drink that does it so well as the Gin Fizz.

But there is one skeleton lurking in the Gin Fizz's cocktail cabinet: the Tom Collins. From an ingredient perspective, the Tom Collins and Gin Fizz are identical. Only their construction differs. For years the bartending elite and cocktail historians have debated whether they should be stirred, shaken, include egg white, and be served over ice.

The historical similarities of these drinks have necessitated some gentle deviation from their original forms. With that in mind, a Tom Collins should be built over ice and simply stirred. A Gin Fizz should be shaken and served with no ice, topped with soda and, crucially, contain egg white. The inclusion of the egg white (for texture) means you have to shake for decent periods of time, and to shake the drink twice. In past times, bartenders would call upon a 'dry shake' to achieve the best possible degree of aeration. This involved shaking the drink without ice first, to whip the cocktail up, then shaking with ice afterwards to make it cold. However, I discovered that the better practice was to shake with ice first, then without afterwards, to avoid knocking all the air back out of the drink. Henceforth, the 'reverse dry shake' became the way. I now see bartenders all over the world doing it.

Better still than dry shaking is blending or foaming the drink. Blending creates a super creamy, super cold version of the Gin Fizz. Aerating the drink in a cream whipper is even better though, as it's easier to control the dilution and maximize fizz.

FRENCH 75

35 ML/1¼ FL. OZ. G'VINE FLORAISON GIN
10 ML/2 TEASPOONS LEMON JUICE (PULP REMOVED)
5 ML/1 TEASPOON SUGAR SYRUP
CHAMPAGNE

Method 1

Premix the gin, lemon and sugar then pop it in the fridge for
1–2 hours. This means that no ice is needed, alleviating any dilution
of flavour. Once cold, measure the premix into the glass and
top up with chilled Champagne.

Method 2

If you have a soda siphon to hand, it's worth the effort of premixing
and chilling (see method 1), and then carbonating everything
(except the Champagne) by charging the siphon with CO_2. Mix the
two fizzy (and chilled) components together in the correct
proportions to finish the drink.

Method 3

Don't worry if the ingredients are warm or cold – simply build
everything into the glass, then add a few pellets of dry ice. The dry
ice will chill and carbonate the cocktail without inflicting any
dilution at all. A few things to be wary of though; dry ice will add
a very subtle acidity to the drink as it releases carbonic acid during
the sublimation process – you can account for this by using 10%
less lemon juice. Also, you must wait until all the dry ice has
'dissolved' away before enjoying the cocktail – don't eat it!

Garnish with a twist of lemon, or a cocktail cherry.
Or both. Or neither.

Let's get one thing straight: Sparkling wine is not an easy ingredient to mix with. Be it Champagne, Cava, Prosecco or indeed any other regionally delineated bubbly – these wines tend not to play nicely with others. This is partly down to the simple fact that sparkling wines are designed to be stand-alone ingredients, not intended for jumbling-up with extraneous flavours. And on this matter they tend to be fairly inflexible, playing on their reputation as the highest-calibre of liquid refreshment: pristine and untouchable. It is ironic then, that the other reason that Champagnes and other fizzy wines don't mix well with other ingredients is because they actually don't taste that great in the first place.

No need to re-read that last bit. Most people recognise the fact that Champagne isn't especially tasty stuff, but choose to happily push on knocking it back because it's the socially correct thing to do. Wait, you don't like Champagne?! No – not especially.

Sure, I'll drink it – because it's wet, contains alcohol, and I'll admit I get a sadistic kick out of knowing that someone (who isn't me) has spent a lot of money buying a bottle of liquid that is, on reflection, of quite inferior quality and complexity to a similarly priced whisky, rum, brandy, Tequila or gin. Or a similarly priced flat wine for that matter. But the truth is, in this author's opinion at least, Champagne is not worthy of either the reverence or the price tag that it receives.

With that little rant behind us, you might now be wondering what to do with that no-longer-so-appealing 'save it for a celebration' bottle of fizz that's been lurking in your cooler for months now. The simple solution is to make a French 75. Or make a few.

There are only a handful of decent sparkling wine-based cocktails known to mankind, and while I'd be happy to concede that the Bellini and Kir Royal are also both good drinks, the simplicity of their construction makes for a less than credible claim of cocktail-hood. The French 75 on the other hand is without doubt a cocktail, and perhaps the only cocktail containing sparkling wine that can truly be deemed delicious. Indeed, the ingredients in this drink don't just pair nicely with one another, they actually taste better than the sum of their parts. Gin, lemon and sugar transform sparkling wine into the liquid that you'll probably end up wishing was in the Champagne bottle in the first place.

There's no particular genius behind this marriage of flavours – the drink is the forehead-slappingly obvious evolution of the Fizz and Sour. Here though, the wine takes the place of the soda. Sounds innocent enough, but when you consider a world where soda water has an alcohol content in excess of 16%, you don't need to be a mathematician to realise that a French 75 packs a bit of a punch.

Putting the theory to the test, after your third French 75 it becomes worryingly evident why the drink was named after a 75-mm (3-inch) field gun. Used to great effect by the French during World War I, and more of a canon than a gun, 'Soixante-Quinze' would fire noxious gas canisters the size of your forearm into enemy trenches. Perhaps it was the explosive and intoxicating effects of Champagne and gin that caused Harry McElhone, the bartender generally credited with the drink's invention, to name his cocktail after the most deadly weapon of the era.

Temperature and fizz are the two major obstacles to overcome when mixing one of these, and with that in mind, there are three different methods that can be employed here, all of them simple but some requiring specialist kit. Naturally the fizz will be softened by the non-carbonated ingredients (yet another reason that sparkling wine cocktails tend to be a let-down), so using a fresh bottle of Champagne is paramount.

GIMLET

60 ML/2 FL. OZ. PLYMOUTH NAVY–STRENGTH GIN
20 ML/⅔ FL. OZ. ROSE'S LIME CORDIAL OR FRESH LIME JUICE

Shake and strain into a freezing cold Martini glass, then devour like you've just been diagnosed with scurvy. You may choose to garnish it with a lime wedge, but I find one an unnecessary distraction.

Back in 1740 a British Admiral by the name of Vernon took the unprecedented step of watering down his sailors' rum rations with citrus juice. While initially (and quite understandably) not a hit with the men, this simple act went on to save countless lives. Seven years later, in 1747, a Scottish surgeon named James Lind discovered that incorporating fruit juice into the sailors' diets dramatically reduced the chances of them contracting a potentially lethal bout of scurvy. It turned out that scurvy was a result of vitamin C deficiency, so all ships began carrying citrus juice. In 1867 it became mandatory for British ships to carry lime-juice rations.

The problem was that the juice tended to go off after a week or two sitting in a barrel. Another enterprising Scotsman, Lauchlan Rose, developed and patented a new method of preserving lime juice by concentrating it. Crucially though, the medicinal properties of the juice were retained and the vitamin C remained intact. Rose's Lime Cordial was born – the world's first concentrated fruit juice.

Drinking lime cordial on its own is no fun at all, so a (very large) spoon-full of gin is necessary to help the medicine go down. The story goes that it was Sir Thomas Gimlette, a surgeon in the Royal Navy, who allegedly introduced this drink as a means of inducing his messmates to take lime juice as an anti-scurvy medication. There's very little in the way of evidence to actually back this story

up, though, and it's more likely that the drink simply takes its name from the sharp handheld tool used for punching holes in things – a description that is just as apt for the drink as it is for the tool.

There's an elephant in the room among bartenders when it comes to mixing gimlets, and that is whether to use fresh lime and sugar, or lime cordial?

As we have already learned, the original calls for Rose's cordial, but the nomination of cordial was driven more by circumstance than by the pursuit of deliciousness. I'd wager lime juice would have been preferable if it were as practical and readily available as it is today. So with that in mind, it's fair to consider a lime juice an upgrade. But this is beginning to sound a lot like a 'Gin Daiquiri', and in the Gimlet we have a cocktail that deserves its own name and its own terms and conditions. For me this is one occasion where nostalgia wins the day, and I'm happy to sacrifice a little freshness in a Gimlet to know that I am drinking a simple union of ingredients that have remained relatively unchanged for over 250 years. A win for Lauchlan Rose!

Now that we have settled upon the ingredients, ratio remains the final point of contention. *The Savoy Cocktail Book* (1930) suggests 50/50 gin and lime cordial, backed up by the 1953 Raymond Chandler novel *The Long Goodbye*, which stated that 'a real gimlet is half gin and half Rose's lime juice and nothing else'. But I urge you to consider what your dentist might say, and lower the lime cordial a little. Three parts gin to one part cordial is a sweeter (or not) spot to aim for.

SALTED LIME RICKEY

50 ML/2 FL. OZ. PLYMOUTH GIN
15 ML/½ FL. OZ. LIME JUICE
1 G/¹⁄₃₂ OZ. SALT
SODA, TO TOP UP

This drink needs to be cold – like, really cold. If possible use glasses from the freezer and make sure that your ice is dry. Fill a highball glass with chunks of ice; add the gin, lime and salt, then give it a good stir with a bar spoon. While still stirring, pour the soda water in, leaving a small space at the top. Add more ice, stir some more, then finish with a wedge of lime.

On page 57 of *Daly's Bartender's Encyclopedia*, published in 1903, a passage reads: 'This drink was devised by the late Colonel Rickey, whose fame as a congenial friend and dispenser of hospitality, as well as a judge of appetizing edibles and liquid refreshments, is world-wide, and it is universally conceded that for a drink containing an alcoholic ingredient it is the most refreshing known.'

This was the first book to publish a recipe for a Gin Rickey but, as the author alludes to, it was already a very popular drink by then and quite possibly the most popular gin-based cocktail of the 1890s. Today however, the Rickey is not known by many and very rarely called for, at least in my experience. It has faded into obscurity, and I'll be the first to admit that for a great deal of my early bartending career, I spared very little thought for the Rickey. It's a Collins or a Fizz made with lime juice, I thought. That's not to say I didn't think

it was tasty – gin, lime and soda is a union of ingredients that makes as much sense on paper as it does swishing down your throat – but the thought of drinking one didn't exactly fill me with excitement. My opinion changed during a trip to India in 2011.

The Rickey is one of the most popular cocktails in India which, given the country's past dealings with gin and the favourability of its climate to citrus fruit growers, should come as no great surprise. But Rickeys are not made in the Western manner out there, oh no. In India, there's either little or no sugar in the recipe and salt is added instead. Salt has the effect of buffering the acidity of the lime juice (in the same way as sugar), but also exposing some minerality from the gin and lime oil. Removing the sugar also makes the drink less cloying and circumvents that nauseating sugar overload that typically happens after about your third or fourth sour/fizzy drink. Putting flavour to one side, forgoing the sugar altogether is an attractive proposition for some, making the drink a friend of diabetics and those counting calories. Although your doctor may question the logic of replacing sugar with salt, Indians swear by the drink's hydrating power during hot summer days.

The Rickey was probably first made with Bourbon, which is a little odd since Bourbon and soda are not especially enthusiastic bedfellows and it'll need a lot more than a squeeze of lime to change that. Nonetheless, George A. Williamson of Shoomaker's bar in Washington thought the marriage a loving one, and at some time in the 1880s conceived the Rickey, naming it after the Democratic lobbyist, Joe Rickey, who may or may not have had some part to play in the drink's creation. One thing is for sure, though: Rickey was quite displeased at having loaned his name to a popular cocktail, once saying that 'I was Col. Rickey, of Missouri, the friend of senators, judges and statesmen and something of an authority on political matters... But am I ever spoken of for those reasons? I fear not. No, I am known to fame as the author of the "rickey," and I have to be satisfied with that.'

PURL

FOR THE BOTANICAL INFUSION
150 ML/5 FL. OZ. PLYMOUTH GIN
3 G/¾ OZ. CRUSHED BLACK PEPPER
3 G/¾ OZ. BAY LEAVES · 3 G/¾ OZ. SAGE
1 G/¹⁄₃₂ OZ. GENTIAN ROOT
1 G/¹⁄₃₂ OZ. WORMWOOD · 1 G/¹⁄₃₂ OZ. STAR ANISE
1 G/¹⁄₃₂ OZ. NUTMEG · 1 G/¹⁄₃₂ OZ. DRIED ROSEMARY

For the botanical infusion, macerate all the ingredients in a jam jar (or similar) for 2 weeks, then strain and reserve. You can speed this process up a little by pressurizing the ingredients in a hand-held cream whipper, charged with a nitrous-oxide cartridge.

FOR THE DRINK (MAKES 700 ML/24 FL. OZ.)
150 ML/5 FL. OZ. BOTANICAL INFUSION (SEE ABOVE)
500 ML/17 FL. OZ./2 CUPS BROWN ALE
50 G/¼ CUP DEMERARA SUGAR
50 G/¼ CUP CASTER/SUPERFINE SUGAR

For the drink, build all the ingredients into a glass bottle or a large jar, allowing the sugar to dissolve. The cocktail can be enjoyed cold, straight from the fridge, or warmed up in its bottle. Adjust the sugar according to taste and feel free to play around with different styles of beer.

I could hardly pen this book without sparing a thought for Purl – the drink that lent its name to my first cocktail bar. Before Purl opened in 2010, you would have been hard-pressed to find a bartender who had heard of this drink. Hendrick's Gin saw the genius in the mixture, though, and collaborated with us on a promotion that gained the drink some traction. But its brief period of fame was a far cry from the mid-18th century, where it would have been difficult to walk past moored boats on the Thames without the aroma of warm Purl.

The drink's original form pre-dates English gin by at least 100 years, becoming popular around the turn of the 17th century. The use of hops as a preservative (and bittering agent) for ales was highly uncommon then, which meant that beer spoiled quickly and tasted bland. Resourceful folk pepped up their beers with other herbs and spices, and wormwood was amongst the most common of these pre-hop seasonings. Beer with wormwood was often called 'Purl' – a 16th century word used to describe the meandering of a stream.

In winter, it became trendy to warm this mixture up, and sometimes seasonal spices and sugar were added. The early, debauched years of the 18th century saw Purl fortified with a healthy measure of the ubiquitous spirit of the age: gin. The drink is celebrated in a handful of Charles Dickens' novels, most notably *The Old Curiosity Shop* (1840) where Dick Swiveller serves a maid 'a great pot, filled with some very fragrant compound, which sent forth a grateful steam, and was indeed choice purl...' The recipe itself is amenable to poetic license and, like mulled wine, can be tailored to your desired level of sweetness and spice. The only ingredients you must use are beer, gin and wormwood, but I'd suggest some sugar to balance the bitterness, and some choice fruits and spices wouldn't go amiss either.

Avoid holding the liquid on the heat too long and don't boil it. I suggest mulling the beer together with sugar and other seasonings for 10 minutes with the lid on, then adding the gin to temper the heat and fortify the mixture. Perhaps the best way is to batch a mixture in sealed bottles, then warm it in a hot water-bath or pan.

⚬⚬ CLOVER CLUB ⚬⚬

FOR THE RASPBERRY SYRUP
250 G/2 CUPS FRESH RASPBERRIES · 2 G/¹⁄₁₆ OZ. SALT
250 G/1¼ CUPS CASTER/SUPERFINE SUGAR
250 ML/1 CUP WATER

Toss the raspberries in the salt and sugar then place in a 1-litre (35-fl. oz.) mason jar (you can also use a zip-lock bag) and pop it in the fridge overnight. In the morning add the water to the jar. Using a temperature probe, bring a saucepan of water up to 50°C (122°F) and turn the temperature right down so that it holds there. Pop the mason jar in the water and leave it for 2 hours, giving it the occasional wiggle. When the 2 hours are up, carefully remove the jar, then strain the contents through a sieve/strainer. You may need to strain a second time using muslin/cheesecloth. To prolong the lifespan of your syrup it's often useful to add a splash of gin or vodka. Store in the fridge for up to 1 month.

CLOVER CLUB
40 ML/1½ FL. OZ. GIN (DARNLEY'S VIEW OR ANY GIN WITH A SPICY KICK)
15 ML/½ FL. OZ. LEMON JUICE
15 ML/½ FL. OZ. RASPBERRY SYRUP
15 ML/½ FL. OZ. MARTINI EXTRA DRY VERMOUTH
15 G/½ OZ. EGG WHITE

Shake all the ingredients with ice, then strain into a separate mixing glass or shaker and shake again with no ice. This 'dry shake' has the effect of whipping air into the cocktail. Strain into a chilled coupe glass and drink it quickly. You can leave the egg white out if you prefer, but it adds a lovely sherbet effect to the palate.

Part gin sour, part Martini, part raspberry liqueur, the Clover Club is fruity, dry, delicate and fiendishly addictive. I think it has something for everyone and, had it been given a chance, I believe it could quite possibly have single-handedly saved the 1980s from the depths of drinking depravity.

The cocktail was named for and enjoyed by members of the eponymous Philadelphia-based lawyers' and writers' club founded in 1882. Like many other gentleman's clubs of the time, a signature drink was an essential component of congenial gatherings. The Clover Club drink dates to 1896, as seen in the 1897 book, *The Clover Club of Philadelphia*.

When I first became a bartender, the Clover Club was still dragging itself out of 70 years worth of obscurity. We used to make them with gin, grenadine, lemon and egg white. It was basically a pink gin sour, and even though it tasted nice enough, it wasn't going to be winning any awards for innovation. The earliest recipe in fact calls for raspberry syrup, not grenadine, and also a splash of vermouth. Slowly, we bartenders began to embrace the classic version, and like the unfurling of pink petals, the beauty and balance of the true Clover Club blossomed.

And for me, it's the addition of a splash a vermouth that really sets the Clover Club apart, where aromatics of thyme and the bitterness of wormwood intercept the raspberry before it becomes overly fruity. That said, the raspberry syrup is probably the most important ingredient. As is often the way with off-the-shelf syrups, most taste more like the devil's confectionery than the carefully concentrated essence of a piece of fresh fruit. Fortunately, raspberry syrup is super-simple to make at home, so I've included the only recipe you'll ever need – it's a game changer as far as the Clover Club is concerned.

NEGRONI

30 ML/1 FL. OZ. GIN
(AVOID CITRUS-FORWARD GINS, THEY GET LOST)
30 ML/1 FL. OZ. CAMPARI
30 ML/1 FL. OZ. NARDINI ROSSO VERMOUTH

A good Negroni should be served over big chunks of freezer-temperature ice, and there's nothing wrong with building the whole thing in a rocks glass. Stir for a full minute, then garnish with a small strip of grapefruit zest or a slice of orange.

For new initiates it's wise to start with Aperol instead of Campari – it's like Campari's better-natured, mawkish cousin. If the bitterness is still too much you can always drop the ratio slightly, or do what I do and just up the gin!

It's a fairly well-kept secret that bartenders don't usually drink cocktails when sat on the receiving end of the bar, preferring instead to swig a beer or down a shot. It's an act of martyrdom, graciously sparing their fellow bartender the ordeal of cocktail mixing and the indignity of being observed by a keeper of the craft. The Negroni is one acceptable deviation from this rule, however. Uncomplicated, yet challenging; strong, yet quaffable, the Negroni is hallowed ground to the bartender – an impeccable decoction of spirit, wine and bitter; blood red and ice cool.

If the significance of the Negroni should ever come into question, one need only observe the openness of bar room discussion about the drink. Everyone has an opinion on its components, method of mixing, garnish and ice; those that swear by it will do so until their dying sip, those that come to dislike it will lay down their lives to avoid a single drop. And even though the brazen character

of the Negroni may divide opinion, it is a drink that all cocktail enthusiasts desperately want to appreciate to its full extent. Regardless of preference, there remains a right of passage, or entitlement when it comes to the Negroni. Like your first face-scrunching sip of wine or beer, the conspiracy that surrounds this drink demands that you try, try again until life become incomplete without it. Here, in the Negroni, is the drink that, beyond all others, has become the Ferrari-red pin-up of the craft cocktail movement.

My understanding of the origins of the Negroni comes from the book *Sulle Tracce del Conte* (On the Trail of the Count) (2002) by Luca Picchi. Backed up by considerable historical documentation, it intimates that the drink is named after ★deep breath★ Camillo Luigi Manfredo Maria Negroni, who originally asked Fosco Scarselli, bartender at Café Casoni, to fortify his Americano (a bitter Italian aperitivo mixed with sweet vermouth and a splash of soda) with gin. This happened at some point in 1919 or 1920. One of the ways in which the story is qualified is by a letter sent from Frances Harper of London to [the evidently unwell] Negroni on October 13th 1920:

'You say you can drink, smoke, and I am sure laugh, just as much as ever. I feel you are not much to be pitied! You must not take more than 20 Negronis in one day!'

Nobody can drink that many Negronis in a single day, so it's fair to assume that the early version of the drink was either quite small or contained proportionately less gin – or both. These days we default to a Negroni made with equal parts gin, bitter liqueur/amaro, and sweet vermouth. The exact ratio can be tweaked (I prefer it slightly in favour of the gin, but with plenty of dilution) along with the brand of gin, bitter and vermouth. It's the simplicity of the drink coupled with the potential for customization that makes it a prevailing classic.

GIN & JUICE

40 ML/1½ FL. OZ. GIN
100 ML/3½ FL. OZ. CINOTTO

Stir the ingredients with plenty of ice in a highball glass.
Garnish with a wedge of blood orange, or a normal orange
if you can't be bothered.

'What the hell is gin and juice?' That was the question I asked
myself before tackling this recipe. It seems like a stupid question,
but when you contemplate it, the whole concept seems a bit odd
– like lathering tomato ketchup on your sushi.

To me, Gin & Juice has always felt like an amusing piece of
alliteration rather than a drink that you would actually mix, let
alone order. When, in 1999, the drink was catapulted to stardom
by rapper Snoop Dogg's rhythmic utterance of the immortal words
'sippin on gin and juice, laid back, with my mind on my money and
my money on my mind', I immediately assumed that Gin & Juice
was a metaphor for something sexual or drug-related. It turns out
it wasn't. It also turns out that America loves Gin & Juice and that,
as a nation, America mixes more gin with juice than it does with
tonic water.

Of course, mixing gin with fruit juices is no new thing. Gin Palaces
were known to sell a drink called a 'Gin Twist', which was made
with lemon juice garnished with a lemon twist, and the near
150-year-old Gimlet (pages 157–159) is little more than gin and
fruit juice concentrate mixed together. Then there's the Red
Snapper (essentially a Bloody Mary with gin), which finds its
origins in the mid-20th century. And the Spanish 'Pomada', which
sees gin traditionally mixed with lemon juice. Gin gets mixed with

juice in Fizzes, Collins, Daisies, Rickeys, Punches and so on. But with those drinks, it is always as a measured souring agent, rather than a lengthener or mixer.

Delving deeper into the practices of Gin & Juice advocates, I found that gin gets mixed with all kinds of different juices, but grape, grapefruit and orange are the most popular choices. Orange and grapefruit make a good fit in theory, given that they crop up regularly in the botanical bill of many London Dry gins. But it doesn't work, or at least not how I would hope it would. The juice kills the gin so that it might as well be vodka that you're mixing, leading back to the conclusion that it's the alliteration on the 'g' and the 'j' that has popularized this drink rather than any deep affinity between the ingredients.

So now it's time to own up, dear reader. I will not be furnishing you with a recipe for gin mixed with fruit juice because it doesn't taste very good. Instead I am suggesting you mix your gin with cinotto. Now, cinotto is not a fruit juice, but it isn't all that far off. Bright red in colour and lightly sparkling, cinotto is a non-alcoholic Italian aperitivo that is also sold under the brand name 'Cino'. It's made from a combination of bitter spices, fruit and sugar and sits somewhere between Campari, blood orange juice and tonic water on the flavour spectrum. Sounds delicious, right? Well, it is. And it's a great match for gin, especially when sat on the porch in your high-tops.

The drink pictured on the previous page was one of my early attempts to emulsify fruity essential oils into gin, sugar, acids and water, effectively constructing a soft drink from scratch. After hitting upon a formula that worked really well, I was struck by the realisation that I had created a soft drink that already existed (albeit with a different colour) – cinotto!

HOLLAND HOUSE

50 ML/1¾ FL. OZ. BOLS GENEVER
20 ML/⅔ FL. OZ. DRY VERMOUTH
10 ML/⅓ FL. OZ. LEMON JUICE
5 ML/1 TEASPOON MARASCHINO LIQUEUR

Shake all the ingredients with ice and strain into a punch glass.
Add an ice cube from a shaker, or use a chunk of clear ice.
Garnish with a lemon twist.

Those readers old enough to remember the manned Moon landings might recall the Holland House brand of cocktail mixer. These popular bottles of 'Whiskey Sour' and 'Daiquiri' mix sought to simplify cocktail mixing at home by giving you all the ingredients you needed (except the alcohol) in one bottle. They enjoyed quite a bit of success in the 1950s and 1960s until people realised that they tasted dreadful. And so began two decades of Dark Ages for the cocktail.

In this book, with its select collection of cocktails, the Holland House serves as a handy mashup of at least three other classic gin cocktails. The first of those is the Martinez, the elder sibling of the Martini and cocktail that I featured in *The Curious Bartender: The Artistry & Alchemy of Creating the Perfect Cocktail*, where the Holland House borrows vermouth and maraschino liqueur. The second is The Aviation, a drink that also featured in my first book, which sees gin combined with lemon juice and maraschino or violet liqueur. The third is the Corpse Reviver No. 2 (favoured child of the

Corpse Reviver family), where we find gin, lemon, orange liqueur and dry vermouth in concert with one another. Fourth – if I may – is the Clover Club and you can turn to pages 166–168 to discover the similarities for yourself.

All of the aforementioned drinks are, in isolation, quite different beasts, despite having a few similar ingredients. The Holland House is like a missing link between them all, probably pre-dating all but the Martinez. In fact, some cocktail buffs argue that the Holland House *is* a Martinez, given the similarities between the widely accepted modern recipe and Jerry Thomas' original Martinez recipe from 1862, which called for: maraschino, Old Tom gin, vermouth, bitters and a slice of lemon – forgo the bitters and up the lemon and you have yourself a Holland House right there. However, a more likely explanation for the similarities between the two drinks is that most mundane of rationales: coincidence.

For the Holland House Cocktail (if you hadn't guessed already), it's the use of genever in place of gin that makes all the difference. The boldness of a nice oude genever or corenwijn really stands up to the lemon and liqueur, while the vermouth offers some welcome dilution and finesse to the ensemble. I've heard the Holland House described as a 'malty Aviation' in the past, which is a fair description but also an injustice to a cocktail that deserves fair recognition in its own right, rather than loose comparisons to better known, classic cocktails (as I have just done).

SLOE GIN

SOUS VIDE/OSMOSIS METHOD

**500 G/1 LB. 2 OZ. SLOE BERRIES · 250 G/1¼ CUPS CASTER/
SUPERFINE SUGAR · 10 G/⅓ OZ. MALIC ACID
5 G/1 TEASPOON SALT · 500 ML/17½ FL. OZ. GIN**

Using a large zip-lock or vacuum bag, add the sloes, 100 g/½ cup of
the sugar, the acid, and salt. Give it a good shake and a bit of a squash
and leave in the fridge overnight. By morning a lot of the juice will
have leached out. Add the rest of the ingredients, including the gin,
then seal the bag and drop it into a water bath set at 65°C (150°F).
Leave to cook for 3 hours. You can go hotter and quicker, but this is
the best balance of flavour and efficiency for me. Remove the bag and
filter the liquid through a fine-mesh filter and muslin/cheesecloth.
Pour the filtered liquid into a sterile bottle. It should keep for years.

BLENDER METHOD

**500 G/1 LB. 2 OZ. SLOE BERRIES · 100 ML/3½ FL. OZ.
WARM WATER · 500 G/17½ FL. OZ. GIN · 200 G/1 CUP SUGAR
10 G/⅓ OZ. MALIC ACID · 5 G/1 TEASPOON SALT**

Makes approximately 1 litre/34 fl. oz./4 cups

Add the room-temperature sloes, water and most of the gin to a
blender. Blend on a high speed in 10-second bursts for 1–2 minutes,
puréeing everything without the liquid heating up too much. Pass
the purée through a coarse sieve/strainer using the back of a spoon
to push all the juice out. Then pass through a finer sieve/strainer,
doing the same, followed by muslin/ cheesecloth. Use what's left of
the gin to 'wash' any flavour out of the leftover fruit pulp. Add the
sugar, acid and salt and bottle the liqueur. Keep in a warm place for
a few hours until the sugar has completely dissolved. Serve chilled.

Not so long ago the home kitchen was a veritable hive of booze-based activity, as household cookbooks like those published by The Women's Institute will testify. Homemade wines, cordials and liqueurs were as commonplace as homemade bread and jams. Gin was a popular candidate for all manner of fruit infusions, both at home and at the big distillers of the day, who sold lemon- and orange-flavoured gins with some success. These days, flavoured gins have all but died out and despite the emergence of some contemporary gin brands choosing to flavour and sweeten their product, it is only sloe gin that has truly stood the test of time. And the manufacture of sloe gin stands as one of the few alcohol-based culinary crafts that remains a homemade British staple.

Before we dive in head first, though, it's important to stress that on the subject of manufacturing sloe gin, we must tread very carefully indeed. There is no other line of conversation that can send handbag ripples through a Women's Institute tea room like the finer points of gin/fruit infusions. What began as a wholesome household craft is now seen by some as a classical art form, shrouded in superstition and mystery. As for the sloe berry itself, there is a fruit that, to some, holds a position of near divine reverence, reflected in the manner in which it must be treated prior to and during sloe gin preparation.

Some older recipes for sloe gin suggest waiting until after the season's 'first frost' before picking the berries. At first this might seem an attempt at some biodynamic strategy (allowing the heavens to align before foraging for the fruit) and explained away by most as nature's way of softening the fruits skin prior to infusion. Science tells us that the hydrogen cyanide (natural antifreeze) content of the fruit increases during cold snaps and imparts a desirable almond character to the liqueur, similar to bitter almond kernels of apple pips. If hydrogen cyanide sounds a bit dangerous to you, that's because it is. In my experience, the first frost generally lands a little too late in the year anyway and runs the risk of losing the crop altogether. One option is to make your own frost by picking the ripe fruit and briefly freezing them before infusion. I've heard of others who choose to prick the sloe berries one by one before mixing them with the gin, in a process so arduous that it has been clinically proven to gradually erode the mind of its physical capabilities and is now officially classified under the Human Rights Act as a form of prolonged mental torture. Traditionally this is done with one of the thorns from the blackthorn tree from whence the sloes were picked, but a needle will do it just fine, so long as it is made from silver (naturally).

The point is that everyone has their own method that's been handed down from one generation to the next. For better or worse, most people are fairly stubborn when it comes to cherished family recipes and as quaint as this may sound, traditions such as these are often tough nuts to crack when it comes to enforcing some logical culinary processes in to the mix.

I make sloe gin using two different methods. Both work very well and both require very little time. The first is to cook the sloe berries, in gin, sous vide. This means packing both fruit and liquor into a ziplock bag (or vacuum-packing bag) and holding it in a temperature-controlled water bath for a few hours. Afterwards the mixture is strained off and sweetened. This method extracts more bitterness than a cold infusion, which means the liquor can take a touch more sugar, resulting in a more concentrated shot of juice.

My second technique is a 'cold' method and it calls for the use of a blender. It isn't pretty or particularly efficient, and it certainly isn't the way your mother would do it, but it gets the job done quickly and easily. It also makes for a good talking point around the Christmas table. Blending the sloes and gin together makes a fine purée that requires only a short infusion followed by a slightly longer filtering process.

In both methods you'll find you need comparatively fewer sloes and far less finger tapping than in the traditional recipes.

FRUIT CUP

FOR THE FRUIT CUP SYRUP
300 G/1½ CUPS CASTER/SUPERFINE SUGAR
200 G/7 OZ. STRAWBERRIES, THINLY SLICED
150 G/5 OZ. CUCUMBER, SKIN REMOVED, SLICED
30 G/1 OZ. GRAPEFRUIT PEEL · 10 G/⅓ OZ. FRESH MINT
LEAVES · SEVERAL SPRIGS DRIED LAVENDER FLOWERS
300 ML/10 FL. OZ. WATER

Sprinkle the sugar over the strawberries, cucumber, grapefruit, mint and lavender and place in the fridge overnight – this helps to draw the moisture out of the fruit. Add the water, then pour everything into a resealable plastic bag. Heat a pan of water and use a temperature probe to hold it at a steady 55°C (130°F). After 4 hours, remove the bag from the pan and strain the contents through a fine mesh sieve/strainer.

FOR THE FRUIT CUP
200 ML/7 FL. OZ. FRUIT CUP SYRUP · 400 ML/14 FL. OZ.
GORDON'S GIN OR ANY OTHER JUNIPER-FORWARD GIN
400 ML/14 FL. OZ. GANCIA ROSSO VERMOUTH
LEMONADE OR GINGER ALE
SLICED STRAWBERRIES, ORANGES, LAVENDER
SPRIGS AND BAY LEAVES, TO GARNISH

Once the syrup has cooled, mix it with the gin and vermouth. Your Fruit Cup will keep best when stored in the fridge and should remain in good shape for up to 6 months. To construct the finished drink, mix one part fruit cup with two parts lemonade or ginger ale (or both) over plenty of ice. Garnish as if your life depends on it.

At first glance the 'fruit cup' appears to be a family of mixed drink still patiently waiting for their renaissance. But when you consider that the Pimm's brand of aperitif is actually a fruit cup, and indeed, the originator of the genre, it's clear that this category needs no help from anyone. In the UK, Pimm's is associated with sitting outside on a sunny summer's day and specifically the Wimbledon tennis tournament, where drinking the stuff, along with eating strawberries and cream, is more or less mandatory.

The Pimm's No. 1 Cup (known simply as Pimm's) is of particular interest to gin drinkers because it's gin-based. Of course it doesn't taste much like gin, that is, until you try the other Pimm's Cups and learn that each have their own unique character driven by different base spirits.

The garnishing of Pimm's has more recently become a point of contention between purists and the 'more is better camp'. The doctrinaires will tell you that Pimm's should only be decorated with the blue flowers or leaves of the borage shrub, and perhaps a slice of lemon if you're really pushing the boat out. But there is an enormous temptation with Pimm's to throw as much fruit at the drink as possible, and I am certainly guilty of this myself (as shown in the photo on the previous page).

My recipe calls for a fruit cup syrup, which is best made sous vide, using a heated water bath, although a pan of hot water and a digital thermometer will do the job just as well. The syrup is then mixed with gin and sweet vermouth for the finished fruit cup.

Now, while we might not think of it as such, the Pimm's No. 1 Cup (or just 'Pimm's' as it is more commonly known) is in fact a bottled cocktail. The 'Cup' family of drinks were defined on paper by Jerry Thomas in his book *How To Mix Drinks or the Bon Vivant's Companion* (1862), but James Pimm actually developed his recipe back in the 1820s, shortly after opening his first oyster bar in 1823. The fruity, herbal infusion was intended as a digestive aid for patrons who had overindulged on shellfish. It proved popular, as did his growing chain of restaurants, and in 1859 he launched a version of the product that could be sold to other restaurants. That product was called the No. 1 Cup, a name which had stuck on account of Pimm serving the drink in large cups in his restaurants.

No. 6 (vodka) is probably the second most common after No. 1, and it has a much lighter colour to match its less spicy taste. Then there's the No. 3 Cup, which was re-released as the warming 'Pimm's Winter' back in 2008. Finally, there's the No. 2 Cup (Scotch whisky), No. 4 Cup (rum) and No. 5 cup (rye whiskey). If you can find an unopened bottle of the latter three you should buy it – they have been out of production since the 1980s. More recently, Pimm's have released numerous other iterations of the product, featuring other fruity combinations.

Looking at the original No. 1 Cup, we find that it performs a clever flavour balancing act, being dark, warm and spicy, as well as crisp, refreshing and fruity (the only product I can think of that does this better is Coca Cola). When mixed with lemonade, ginger ale, ginger beer or a combination thereof, the liquid really comes alive and it's quite astonishing how many pitchers of the stuff can be demolished over a sunny afternoon's picnic bench. Cucumber sits near the top of that list for me – with its cooling qualities and fresh aroma, British supermarket shelves are often cleared of cucumbers when it turns Pimm's-o-clock.

GLOSSARY

Botanical Anything that grows (fruit, root, bark, seed, herb, flower). Used to flavour London Dry Gin, Distilled Gin and Genever.

Bourbon cask 180–200-litre (48–53-US gallon) charred American oak cask.

Charred (cask) A barrel or cask that as been burnt on the inside with an open flame. This process caramelizes wood sugars and opens the grain of the cask, typically speeding up the maturation process and imparts 'brown' or burnt flavours into a spirit.

Cut/Cutting Can be used in relation to 'cutting' the Heads or Tails of a distillate, or when cutting a distillate with neutral spirit, water etc.

Ester A chemical compound formed by the interaction of an acid and an alcohol. Typically smells fruity and floral.

Floor Malting Traditional process of malting barley, where the grains are spread evenly across a large floor space and regularly turned over typically a week long period (but variable).

GNS Grain Neutral Spirit (see Neutral Spirit).

Heads The first liquid distillate to flow off a still; typically 3–10% of the entire run. The heads are usually discarded because they contain dissolved oils that can make a spirit cloudy in appearance.

Heart The drinkable body of a gin distillation run that comes after the Heads and before the Tails (i.e. the good stuff).

Moutwijn/Malt wine A triple-distilled spirit made from a fermented mash of barley, corn, wheat, or rye, or combination thereof. Malt wine is generally distilled first in a column-style still, then redistilled twice in a pot still. Malt wine can be used in a number of different ways to create jonge, oude, corenwijn, or 100% moutwijn genever. It can also be distilled a fourth time, with juniper or other botanicals.

Neutral Spirit Spirit distilled above 96% ABV and made from cereal, potato, grape, molasses, or any other sugar or starch source. Can be denoted as Grain Neutral Spirit, which infers that cereal is the base product.

Reflux The (repeated) condensing of vapours within a still before it has reached the condenser proper. Reflux is controlled by temperature and time and is one way of producing a lighter spirit.

Supercritical CO$_2$ extraction A process used to extract essential oils and distillates. Carbon dioxide is forced through the medium to be extracted (such as a botanical in solid or liquid form) under very high pressure. The gas becomes too warm to be a liquid and too squashed together to be a gas, so it sits somewhere in the middle: a supercritical fluid. Carbon dioxide in this state is an incredibly powerful solvent and its extremely high pressure – comparable to the pressure at the bottom of an ocean – ensuring that it is forced deep within the cell structure of organic materials.

Tails The low alcohol leftovers of a gin distillation run. Sometimes the Tails are distilled over until the pot is run nearly dry; other times they refer to the slushy mix that is left in the still.

Toasted (cask) A barrel or cask that has been grilled on the inside over a period of time (typically over a minute) by means of radiant heat. This is a less intensive process than charring that imparts softer, baked, nutty, and toasted flavours in to a spirit.

Tannin/tannic Coloured substance extracted from wood that gives a sensation like a drying bitterness on the tongue. Derivatives of gallic acid.

Vapour Infusion A method of botanical flavour extraction wherein spirit passes through a botanical rack or chamber in its vaporous form.

Virgin (wood/oak) A cask/barrel that has not previously held any spirit or wine (i.e. Bourbon, sherry).

Volatile Molecules with evaporative tendencies that distil easily and, assuming they are not odourless, can also be smelled easily.

Wash Alcoholic beer produced from the fermentation of mashed cereals.

INDEX

A
Adam's column 56
ageing, genevers 105
alcohol by volume
    (ABV) 86, 101, 106
America 68–71
angelica 124–7
aroma 101–4, 107–8

B
bay leaves: Purl 163–5
Borovicka 136
botanicals 82, 107–8
    angelica 124–7
    cardamom 114–15
    cinnamon 120–3
    coriander seeds 112–13
    distilled gin 131–2
    juniper 109–11
    liquorice 116–17
    low-pressure
        distillation 95
    multi-shot gins 97–8,
        99
    one-shot gins 97–8
    orris 118–19
    steeping and boiling
        87–8, 90
bottling 104
brown ale: Purl 163–5

C
Campari: Negroni
    169–71
cardamom 114–15
Carter heads 89
casks 105
cereals, genever
    production 105
Champagne: French 75
    153–6
cinchona 60–1, 146,
    149

cinnamon 120–3
cinotto: Gin & Juice
    172–4
classification 130–9
Clover Club 166–8
cocktails 70–1, 72,
    141–85
Coffey Stills 57, 85
column stills 85–6, 89
compounding 99–100
coriander seeds 112–13
cucumber: fruit cup
    182–5
cutting 101–4

D
distillation: craft distilling
    movement 78–9
    distilleries 49–51
    genever 106
    history 12–15, 56–7
    low-pressure
        distillation 95–6
    master distillers 91
    multi-shot gins 97–8,
        99
    neutral spirit 85–6
    new styles 58–9
    one-shot gins 97–8
    re-distillation 84
    steeping and boiling
        87–8, 90
    vapour infusion 89–90
distilled gin, classification
    131–2
Dry Martini 142–5

E
egg whites: Clover Club
    166–8
    Whipper Gin Fizz
    150–2
ethanol 86

F
fermentation, genever
    105–6
flavourings: flavour map
    128–9
    maceration 82–4
    'off-the-shelf' 84
French 75 153–6
fruit cup 182–5
fruit juice: Gin & Juice
    172–4

G
G&T 60, 74, 146–9
genever: classification
    137–9
    history 24–9, 68
    Holland House
    175–7
    production 105–6
gentlemen of gin 48–51
Gimlet 157–9
Gin Acts 44–7, 48
gin and homemade tonic
    146–9
Gin & Juice 172–4
gin craze 38–41
Gin Fizz 150–2
Gin Lane 42–3
Gin de Mahón 135
gin palaces 52–3
grapefruit: fruit cup
    182–5

H
heads 87
heart 87–8
history 11–79
    in 18th century 34–7
    American gin 68–71
    early history 12–15
    fashionable London
        drink 30–3

ABOUT THE AUTHOR

Tristan Stephenson is an award-winning bar operator, bartender, barista, chef, some-time journalist, and bestselling author of the *Curious Bartender* series of drinks books. He is the co-founder of London-based Fluid Movement, a globally renowned drinks consultancy firm, and half the brains behind the drinks programmes at some of the world's top drinking and eating destinations. In 2009 he was ranked 3rd in the UK Barista Championships. He was awarded UK bartender of the year in 2012 and in the same year was included in London Evening Standard's 'Top 1000 most influential Londoners'.

Having started his career in the kitchens of various Cornish restaurants, Tristan moved up to designing cocktails and running bar operations for Jamie Oliver's Fifteen restaurant in Cornwall in 2007. He then worked for Diageo, the world's biggest premium drinks company. After co-founding Fluid Movement in 2009, Tristan opened two bars in London – Purl and the Worship Street Whistling Shop. The latter was awarded *Time Out London*'s best new bar in 2011 and has been placed in the 'World's Fifty Best Bars'. In 2014 Fluid Movement opened Surfside restaurant in Cornwall, which was awarded the No. 1 position in *Sunday Times* 'Best alfresco dining spots in the UK 2015'. Tristan served as head chef for the first year and continues to manage the menus. In 2016 Fluid Movement opened Black Rock (a bar dedicated to whisky), followed in 2017 by The Napoleon Hotel at the same site. It is London's smallest hotel, boasting just one bedroom but three separate bars: The Devil's Darling (a classic cocktail bar), Sack (a sherry and tapas bar) and the original Black Rock bar.

Tristan's first book, *The Curious Bartender Volume I: The Artistry & Alchemy of Creating the Perfect Cocktail*, was published in 2013 and shortlisted for the prestigious André Simon Award. His second book, *The Curious Bartender: An Odyssey of Malt, Bourbon & Rye Whiskies*, appeared in 2014. In 2015 he wrote *The Curious Barista's Guide to Coffee* (having harvested, processed, roasted and brewed the first cup of UK-grown coffee from the Eden Project in Cornwall). For his fourth book, *The Curious Bartender's Gin Palace*, also shortlisted for the André Simon Award, Tristan visited over 150 distilleries in over 20 countries, including Holland, Scotland, Mexico, Cuba, France, Lebanon, Italy, Guatemala,

Japan, America and Spain. His fifth book, *The Rum Revolution,* appeared in 2017 and demonstrated how rum has moved beyond its Caribbean heartlands, with new distilleries appearing in Brazil, Venezuela, Colombia and Guatemala and in unexpected places, such as Australia, Japan, Mauritius and the Netherlands. Tristan's latest project is *The Curious Bartender Volume II: The New Testament of Cocktails* – a follow-up to his original bestselling book. It features classic cocktail recipes plus Tristan's own highly imaginative spins and in-depth explanation of mixology methods.

Tristan's other commercial enterprises include his drinks brand Aske-Stephenson which manufactures and sells pre-bottled cocktails in flavours as diverse as Peanut Butter and Jam Old-Fashioned and Flat White Russian. He has also launched an on-line whisky subscription service, whisky-me.com. In 2017 Tristan joined supermarket chain Lidl UK as a consultant to the buyers on the own-brand spirits range.

Tristan lives in Cornwall and is husband to Laura and father to two small children. In his limited spare time he rides a Triumph motorcycle, designs websites, cooks a lot, attempts DIY tasks, and collects whisky and books.

ACKNOWLEDGMENTS

The biggest thanks, as always, must go to Laura and Dexter for allowing me the time, space and patience to make this book happen.

Big thanks to Tom as well – my other partner in life.

Thanks to the teams at Whistling Shop and Surfside for being generally awesome and for being curious bartenders.

Addie and Sari for tasty photos and their boundless energy for these books.

Thanks once again to Nathan, Geoff and the team at RPS: Julia, Leslie, Gordana and Cindy.

Jake Burger, Jose Carlos, Sam Carter, Hannah Lanfear, Duncan McRae, John Parsons, Tim Stones, Dennis Tamse and Dan Warner, and to Ginge Warneford for putting the 'badass' into ambassador.

Thanks to all the distillers and producers who allowed me to poke and probe their at their operations, in particular: Jamie Baxter, Jared Brown, Kris Dickenson, Nik Fordham, Tarquin Leadbetter, John McCarthy, Charles Maxwell, Tom Nichol, Desmond Payne, Darren Rook, Nick Strangeway and Gilbert Van Zuidam. Phillip Duff for help with Genever.

Finally, Walter and Lucy Riddel, thanks for allowing me into your home and serving me lobster.

Ian and Hilary Hart, for allowing me into your home and serving me cyanide.

PICTURE CREDITS